Story Friends™

TEACHER GUIDE

by

Howard Goldstein
University of South Florida
Tampa

and

Elizabeth Spencer Kelley
University of Missouri-Columbia

PAUL H. BROOKES PUBLISHING CO.®

Baltimore • London • Sydney

·P A U L·H·
BROOKES
PUBLISHING Co.®

Paul H. Brookes Publishing Co.
Post Office Box 10624
Baltimore, Maryland 21285-0624
USA

www.brookespublishing.com

Story Friends MILLIE™ MULTITIERED INTERVENTIONS FOR LANGUAGE & LITERACY IN EARLY CHILDHOOD

Typeset by Absolute Services Inc., Towson, Maryland.
Manufactured in China by Nordica.

Illustrations by Andrew Friz.

Library of Congress Cataloging-in-Publication Data

The Library of Congress has cataloged the print edition as follows:

Names: Goldstein, Howard, 1953- author. | Kelley, Elizabeth Spencer, author.
Title: Story Friends™ Teacher Guide / by Howard Goldstein and Elizabeth Spencer Kelley.
Description: Baltimore : Paul H. Brookes Publishing, Co., [2016] | Includes bibliographical references.
Identifiers: LCCN 2016000450 | ISBN 9781681251318 (pbk.)
Subjects: LCSH: Language arts (Preschool)
Classification: LCC LB1140.5.L3 .G65 2016 | DDC 372.6—dc23
LC record available at http://lccn.loc.gov/2016000450

British Library Cataloguing in Publication data are available from the British Library.

2020 2019 2018 2017 2016
10 9 8 7 6 5 4 3 2 1

Program Authors

Howard Goldstein, Ph.D., CCC-SLP

Dr. Howard Goldstein is Associate Dean of Research and Professor of Communication Sciences and Disorders in the College of Behavioral and Community Sciences at University of South Florida in Tampa. He is a certified speech-language pathologist. His contributions to the field were recognized as a Fellow of the American Speech-Language-Hearing Association (ASHA) in 1989. He has served ASHA as a member, site visitor, trainer, and chair of a number of task forces and committees related to treatment efficacy, the Ph.D. shortage in the field, practice and policies related to mental retardation and developmental disabilities, academic issues and accreditation, and clinical practice research. He served as the ASHA Vice President for Science and Research, 2013–2015.

Dr. Goldstein is a nationally known scholar for his research in the field of child language intervention research. His research has sought to improve the communication and social skills of children with autism and other developmental disabilities. His recent work has sought to enhance the language and literacy development of students in high-poverty schools who are at high risk for language and reading disabilities. He has authored two books and more than 100 scholarly journal articles and book chapters. Dr. Goldstein has participated in more than 40 research and personnel preparation grants, and he has served as Principal Investigator for more than 30 sponsored projects and on numerous editorial boards and grant review panels.

Elizabeth Spencer Kelley, Ph.D., CCC-SLP

Dr. Elizabeth Spencer Kelley is an Assistant Professor of Communication Science and Disorders in the School of Health Professions at the University of Missouri–Columbia. She is a certified speech-language pathologist. Dr. Kelley's research focuses on language and early literacy skills in young children with limited oral language skills. Her recent work has sought to identify effective approaches for vocabulary intervention for preschool children. In addition, she has conducted projects to examine word learning in young children with oral language difficulties.

Acknowledgments

Work on this projected was conducted by the Center for Response to Intervention in Early Childhood and supported by Cooperative Agreement R324C080011 from the National Center for Special Education Research, Institute of Education Sciences, U.S. Department of Education. We are grateful for the insightful input and feedback provided by our many collaborators, Charlie Greenwood, Judy Carta, Scott McConnell, Ruth Kaminski, and their staff members at the University of Kansas, the University of Minnesota, and the Dynamic Measurement Group. School personnel as well as children and families in Columbus, Ohio; Tampa, Florida; and Kansas City, Missouri and Kansas, were instrumental in our curriculum development work. We had the good fortune to work with an amazing cadre of students and professionals who contributed to the hard work and fun of creating stories, illustrations, and interventions; producing and designing our books and audio narration; administering the various versions of the curriculum; training school staff and research assistants; and evaluating the effects of what became the *Story Friends™* curriculum.

Contents

Program Overview

What Is *Story Friends*?

Story Friends™ is a research-based, supplemental Tier 2 intervention program for use in preschool and kindergarten classrooms. The program includes interactive storybooks and audio recordings used together to develop vocabulary, concepts, and comprehension skills. At small group listening centers, children listen to recorded stories and lessons that encourage interactive responses. During each 10- to 15-minute session, children listen to a story, engage in vocabulary activities, and respond to comprehension questions that promote critical thinking.

Story Friends Is Easy and Fun to Implement in Your Classroom!

The *Story Friends* program is designed to work in the preschool or kindergarten classroom by fitting into a typical early childhood schedule and requiring minimal advanced preparation—the instruction is all prerecorded. Simply add the program to your daily center rotation or small group time. Children will enjoy the stories, likable characters, and colorful illustrations.

Story Friends Components at a Glance

Storybooks

Audio Recordings

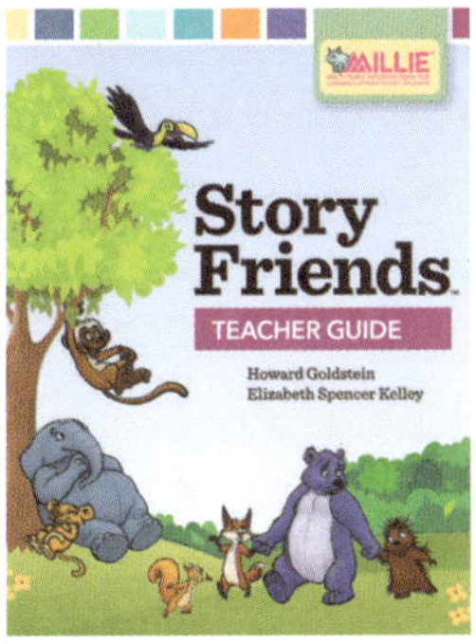

Teacher Materials

Professional Development Modules

Story Friends Employs Best Practices to Accelerate Skills Development

Children who participate in *Story Friends* develop oral language skills and acquire challenging vocabulary. They also practice listening comprehension by responding to questions about stories and characters to help develop their critical thinking skills. In addition to vocabulary growth, children gain experience with academic activities common in preschool and kindergarten settings that employ best practices for learning.

Skills

- Oral language
- Vocabulary
- Comprehension
- Critical thinking
- Listening
- Phonological awareness
- Concepts of print
- Social-emotional

Best Practices

- Explicit teaching and modeling
- Repeated readings
- Multiple exposures to vocabulary
- Student engagement
- Small group intervention
- Recursive instruction
- Formative and summative assessments
- Staff development

Research Base for *Story Friends*

Although *Story Friends* has wide appeal to young children, the embedded lessons in the stories are designed to promote language development among children who are at risk for reading difficulties due to underdeveloped oral language skills. Thus, the research focused on the effects of the program on vocabulary and oral language development with at-risk prekindergarten populations. Also, teachers have implemented this curriculum with kindergarten children who are exhibiting delays in oral language development with good success.

Children's Vocabulary Acquisition Using the *Jungle Friends* Series

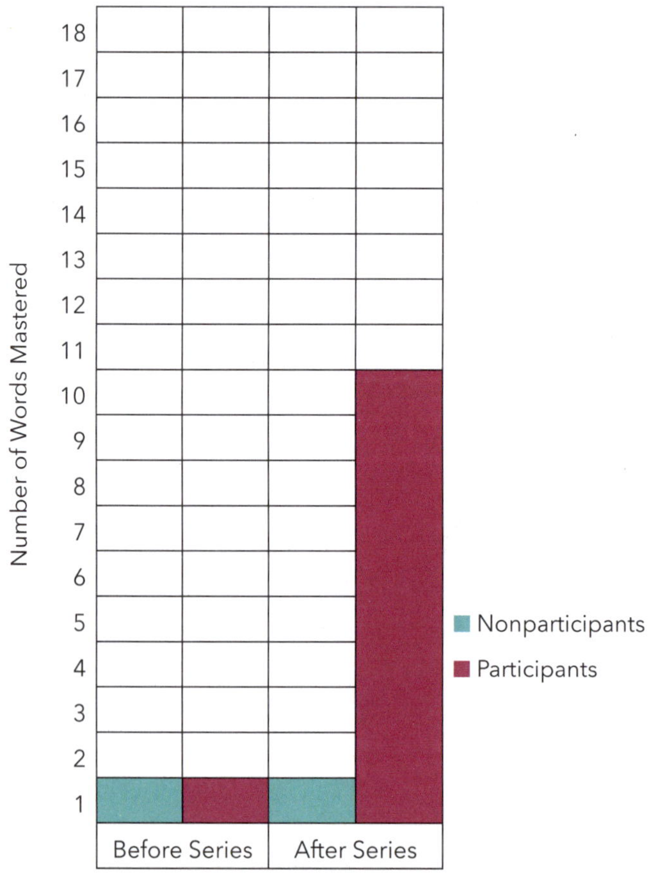

From Research to Practice

Years of research show and experts agree on how curriculum best meets the needs of early childhood skills development and classroom practices.

Preschool Developmental and Programmatic Needs	*Story Friends* Delivers
Language skills	Program vocabulary words with picture supports in each storybook provide child-friendly definitions, multiple opportunities to say the words and definitions, meaning from context, and examples from daily experiences.
Comprehension, critical thinking, and problem-solving skills	Inferential questions from each story challenge children to think critically and problem solve. Intervention lessons model responses, and think-alouds explain reasoning.
Listening skills	Small group listening centers provide opportunities to practice listening skills; visual cues guide children to stay on task and focus their attention.
Phonological awareness	Rhyming story text facilitates learning of an important aspect of phonological awareness.
Concepts of print	Explicit instruction guides children to follow the words of a book's title, turn pages, point to elements in images, and manipulate book flaps on cue.
Social-emotional development	A recurring cast of characters fosters children's social awareness and develops their sense of empathy as they relate to everyday occurrences and social situations.
Explicit teaching and modeling	Child-friendly vocabulary definitions are stated explicitly, and modeling and think-alouds provide context and examples of reasoning for appropriate responses.
Multiple exposures to new vocabulary and language	Children receive four vocabulary and two concept words lessons, as well as guided instruction on three comprehension questions, for a total of nine explicit lessons for each 10- to 15-minute Listening Center session.
Repeated readings	Children listen to each storybook three times to ensure multiple exposures to instruction.
Recursive instruction	Intervention lessons model and guide the acquisition of language skills. Children can listen to other responses and have time to reflect on their own, and children can try out new learning during individual progress monitoring opportunities.
Assessments	Children's progress is monitored during Listening Center sessions to ensure that listening and responding occur appropriately. Individually administered assessments evaluate acquisition of vocabulary and concept words.
Professional development	Teachers have access to multimedia modules to ensure program implementation with fidelity.

Program Components

Student Components

Storybooks

The *Story Friends* program provides two series of storybooks, *Jungle Friends* and *Forest Friends*. The *Story Friends* storybooks showcase:

- Embedded vocabulary
- Colorful, engaging illustrations
- Repeating story characters
- Rhyming text
- "Discovery flaps" that promote natural curiosity and critical thinking

Jungle Friends Series

Forest Friends Series

Multiple Opportunities for Practice

The *Story Friends* program is designed to promote active responding. Children participate by answering questions, pointing to pictures, lifting flaps, and using gestures during pantomime activities. Each storybook provides up to 20 opportunities for active response.

Jungle Friends, Ellie's First Day, pp. 6-7

Vocabulary

Story Friends provides explicit instruction for embedded vocabulary within storybooks. High-level vocabulary develops oral language at an accelerated pace to get children on-level. Each vocabulary lesson includes:

- Child-friendly definitions.
- Opportunities to repeat the words and definitions.
- Opportunities to respond in an interactive format.
- Information about word meaning in context.
- Examples from real-life experiences.

Forest Friends, Fae's Nose Knows, pp. 14-15

Comprehension

Interactive story questions help develop critical thinking and comprehension skills, such as predicting and inferring. Each comprehension lesson includes:

- Sample answers to questions.
- Think-alouds that model reasoning.

Discovery Flaps

Discovery flaps promote natural curiosity as children respond to prompts and interact with images.

Explicit Instruction

Wanda the Word Wolf, the program narrator, appears within storybooks to indicate explicit instruction at point of use.

Audio

Audio Recordings

Wanda the Word Wolf, the program narrator, reads the story text as children follow along. She also delivers explicit vocabulary instruction and comprehension lessons that engage children and promote critical thinking about the text and ideas.

Teacher Components

Teacher Guide

The *Story Friends* Teacher Guide provides everything you need to know about the program and its implementation.

- Program overview and components
- Scope and sequence of skills
- Implementation guidelines
- Audio scripts
- Placement and assessments
- Blackline resource masters
- Research base

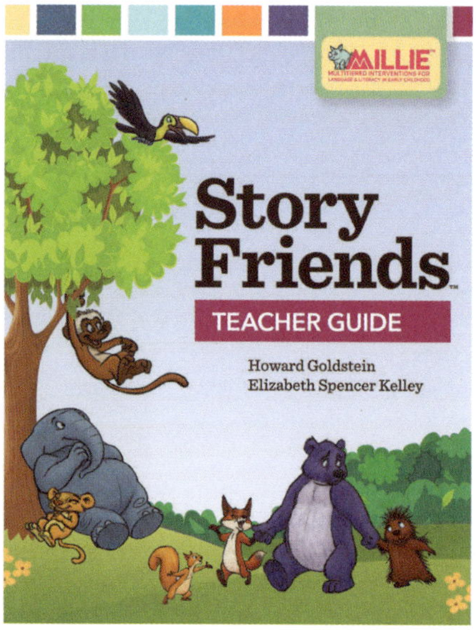

Story Friends Teacher Guide

Program Implementation Modules

Story Friends supports staff development by providing multimedia Program Implementation Modules. These modules illustrate helpful tips for implementing the program with fidelity, ensuring that children in your classroom get the support they need to help them get on-level.

USB Content

The *Story Friends* USB includes the MP3 audio files and full audio scripts that correspond with each of the storybooks. Wanda the Word Wolf narrates each story in the Story Friends series to the children and leads them through the intervention. The USB also contains reproducible and fillable assessment and tracking forms to help monitor children's progress and log children's attendance and pacing of program implementation.

Assessment

The *Story Friends* progress monitoring assessments appear in the Teacher Guide and on the USB and include Unit Vocabulary and Concept Words Assessments. Assessment Cards are included for use with the Concept Words Pre- and Posttests.

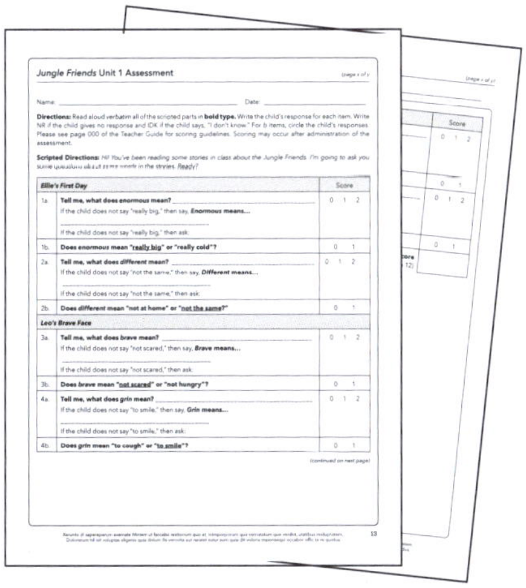

Jungle Friends
Unit 1 Vocabulary Assessment

Unit Vocabulary Assessment

Unit Vocabulary Assessments evaluate children's acquisition of program vocabulary. Children are assessed before and after each instructional unit.

Concept Words Pre- and Posttests

Concept Words Pre- and Posttests evaluate children's acquisition of basic concept words, such as *high* and *low*. Children are assessed before and after each book series, *Jungle Friends* and *Forest Friends*.

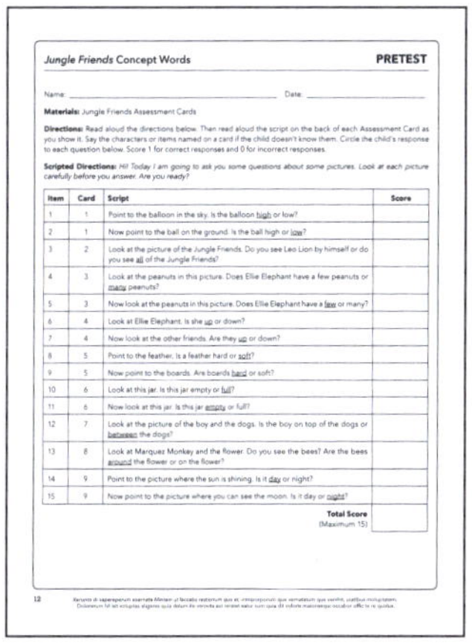

Jungle Friends Concept Words Pretest

Jungle Friends Assessment Cards

Assessment Cards

The Concept Words Assessments use picture cards to assess children's acquisition of basic concept words in an interactive format. Each storybook series, *Jungle Friends* and *Forest Friends*, includes a set of nine Assessment Cards.

Implementing *Story Friends*

An Easy Three-Step Model!

The *Story Friends* program makes it easy for you to implement its Tier 2 supplemental intervention curriculum in three easy steps:

1. **Identify.**
2. **Implement.**
3. **Assess.**

STEP 1 Identify. Identify children who will benefit from using *Story Friends.*

The first step in implementing *Story Friends* is to identify children in your classroom who will benefit from using the program. These will be children who have limited oral language skills or are demonstrating delays in oral vocabulary and comprehension. Information from universal screening and progress monitoring assessments can be used to identify children who are good candidates for using the *Story Friends* supplemental curriculum. You can also use the screening questionnaire provided with this program to identify these children. Please see the *Decision-Making Framework Teacher Questionnaire* on page 115 of this Teacher Guide. For information about other universal screening measures, please see page 82.

STEP 2 Implement. Implement the intervention at the Listening Center.

The *Story Friends* intervention is delivered at the Listening Center in 10- to 15-minute sessions. A facilitator—a teacher or another adult such as an assistant teacher, paraprofessional, or parent—is present to guide and monitor children. At the Listening Center, children follow along as they listen to storybooks and participate in interactive vocabulary and comprehension lessons. Optimally, three children in need of intervention gather at the Listening Center at one time. As it fits within your instructional goals and classroom schedule, you may choose to invite another child to the Listening Center or make it part of every child's routine center rotation or free-choice time. Please see pages 18–21 of this Teacher Guide for information about setting up and operating the Listening Center.

STEP 3 Assess. Administer progress monitoring assessments.

In *Story Friends,* learning of instructional targets is assessed using curriculum-based measures. There are two measures for vocabulary. Vocabulary acquisition is measured using Unit Vocabulary Assessments, administered after four weeks of instruction, and Concept Words Assessments, administered before and after each book series, *Jungle Friends* and *Forest Friends.* Please see pages 10–11 of this Teacher Guide for information about administering the *Story Friends* progress monitoring assessments.

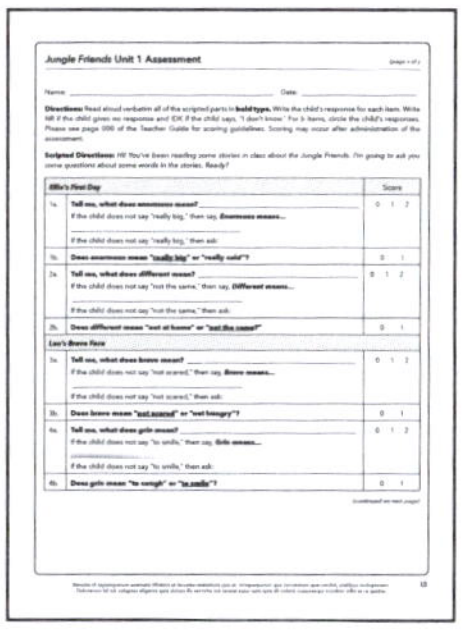

Unit Vocabulary Assessment

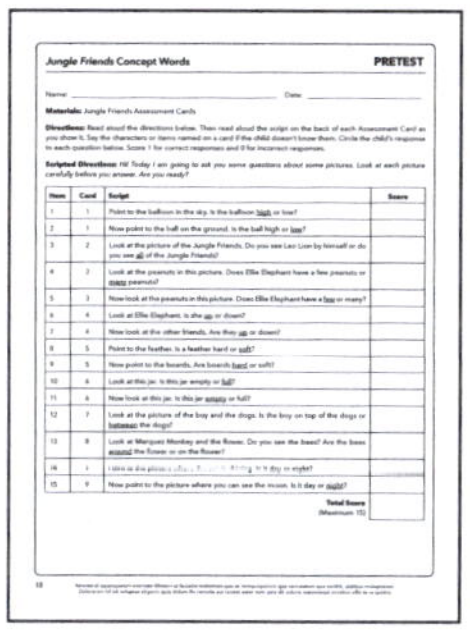

Concept Words Pretest

Program Pacing

Story Friends contains 26 storybooks, each used across a five-day period. Children listen to each storybook three times—one listening session on each of the first three days of your week. Repeated readings of each book ensure that children receive multiple exposures to the rich vocabulary and comprehension instruction.

If a child is absent for a listening session, provide a make-up session on one of the last two days of the five-day period. If a child misses the make-up days, then he or she will join the group for the beginning of the next storybook.

Day 1	Day 2	Day 3	Day 4	Day 5
1st listen	2nd listen	3rd listen	Make-up	Make-up

Use the Attendance Logs provided for each unit of instruction on pages 108–113 of this Teacher Guide to record each time children listen to a storybook and track their progress toward learning goals. Use the Pacing Charts on pages 106–107 of this Teacher Guide to pace your instruction and progress monitoring schedule.

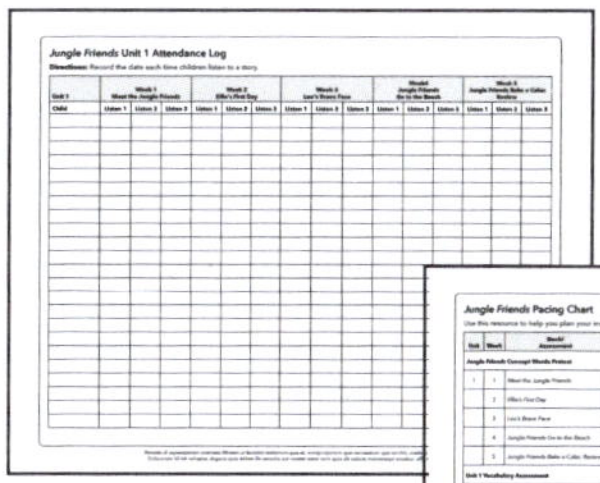

Attendance Log, p. 108

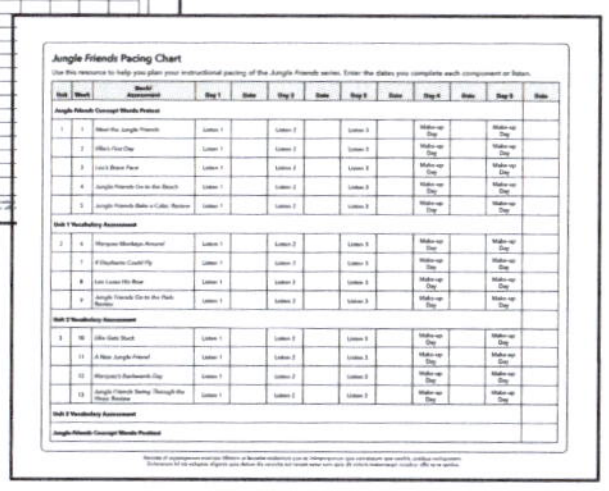

Pacing Chart, p. 106

Key Program Elements

Important Components of *Story Friends* Instruction

The *Story Friends* program provides intensive instruction to maximize children's learning. Lessons are designed to include multiple exposures to content, explicit teaching and modeling, and many opportunities for engagement and practice.

- **Repeated Readings** Children listen to each *Story Friends* book three times. Repeated readings ensure that children receive multiple exposures to rich content. Four vocabulary, three comprehension, and two Concept Words lessons appear in each storybook for a total of nine meaningful instructional opportunities during each 10- to 15-minute listening session.
- **Explicit Teaching** In guided vocabulary lessons, definitions are explicitly stated in child-friendly language. Additional contexts and examples are embedded in "think-alouds" and other modeling of age- and developmentally appropriate reasoning for story questions.
- **Multiple Opportunities for Practice** Children learn best when they are engaged. The *Story Friends* program is designed to promote active responding. Children participate by answering questions, looking at and pointing to pictures, lifting flaps, and gesturing during lesson activities. One storybook provides up to 20 opportunities to respond to vocabulary prompts and comprehension questions.

Instructional Content

Focus on Vocabulary, Concepts, and Comprehension

Although *Story Friends* promotes mastery of many developmentally appropriate skills for preschoolers, the program contains lessons designed to strengthen children's oral language skills, focusing on vocabulary, concept words, and comprehension.

Frequency of Skills Lessons per Storybook

	Skill Load	Teach	Review
Vocabulary	Two vocabulary words	Two introductory lessons	Two review lessons
Concept Words	One or two concept words	One introductory lesson	One review lesson
Comprehension	Three comprehension questions	Three lessons	

- **Vocabulary** In each *Story Friends* instructional book, interactive lessons introduce two new vocabulary words that include explicit, child-friendly definitions and multiple opportunities to respond. The vocabulary words selected for each storybook challenge children to expand their word knowledge in ways that will be useful in a school setting and will have the most impact on their language skills and future reading comprehension. The *Story Friends* vocabulary words are:
  - Relevant to children's daily lives and useful across many content areas.
  - Words that occur frequently in adult conversations and in texts children will encounter in school.
  - Examples of rich language, including descriptive verbs and adjectives that exemplify shades of meaning, such as *leap, search, gorgeous,* and *enormous*.
  - Likely to be unfamiliar to many preschoolers, but provide opportunities for vocabulary expansion.
  - Difficult to learn from context without explicit instruction and multiple exposures.
- **Concept Words** Each *Story Friends* book provides instruction on one or two basic concepts, such as *up/down, many/few,* and *all.* The concept words included in *Story Friends* are selected from preschool curricula and from tests of basic concepts. The concepts are selected to be immediately relevant in the preschool classroom and in future school settings.
- **Comprehension Questions** The *Story Friends* program provides children opportunities to respond to stories and their characters, using comprehension skills. Each storybook prompts children to respond to three comprehension questions. After each prompt, children have time to reflect and respond before hearing a model and the reasoning for an appropriate response.

  The comprehension questions are primarily open-ended, inferential questions for which the answer is not explicitly stated in the text. Children must use information in the story and their own background knowledge to make inferences about character emotions and actions, predictions about future events, and connections to their lives, such as *Why was Ellie excited? Do you think Bobby Bear will be scared the next time he goes to the doctor? Why should you share with your friends?* This critical thinking practice will help prepare children for reading comprehension activities in later grades.

Jungle Friends

Week 1

Meet the Jungle Friends

Introduce the book series and characters.

Ellie Elephant

Marquez Monkey

Leo Lion

Tanisha Toucan

Unit	Week	Book	Vocabulary √	Topics	Comprehension Questions
1	2	*Ellie's First Day* 	enormous different **Concept Words:** high, low	first day of school; making new friends; helping **Feelings:** excitement, embarrassment	▪ Ellie Elephant is excited. Why is Ellie excited? ▪ The other kids laughed at Ellie Elephant. Why did they laugh at Ellie? ▪ At the end of the story, Ellie Elephant was happy. Why was Ellie happy?
	3	*Leo's Brave Face* 	brave grin **Concept Word:** all	going to the dentist **Feelings:** fear, bravery	▪ Leo is afraid. Why is he afraid? ▪ What did Leo Lion learn from the dentist? ▪ Do you think Leo Lion will brush his teeth every night?
	4	*Jungle Friends Go to the Beach* 	gorgeous soaked **Concept Words:** many, few	working together; going to the beach **Feeling:** enjoyment	▪ Tanisha Toucan is happy. Why is Tanisha happy? ▪ At the end of the story, the Jungle Friends worked together. Why should you work together with your friends? ▪ Do you think the Jungle Friends will go to the beach again?
Review	5	*Jungle Friends Bake a Cake* 	grin different enormous gorgeous brave soaked	working together; baking a cake **Feelings:** excitement, happiness	  
2	6	*Marquez Monkeys Around* 	reckless ruin **Concept Words:** up, down	listening to friends **Feelings:** anger, regret	▪ The friends are mad. Why are they mad? ▪ In this story, Marquez Monkey was not being careful. Why should you be careful? ▪ The next time Marquez goes to the jungle, do you think he will swing around wildly?

√ = Tested Skills

Unit	Week	Book	Vocabulary √	Topics	Comprehension Questions
2	7	*If Elephants Could Fly* 	imagine soar **Concept Words:** soft, hard	flying, travel **Feeling:** surprise	▪ Ellie Elephant's little brother is surprised. Why is he surprised? ▪ At the end of the story, Ellie Elephant was glad she cannot fly. Why was she glad? ▪ In this story, Ellie Elephant pretended she could fly. What do you like to pretend?
	8	*Leo Loses His Roar* 	ill comfort **Concept Words:** empty, full	being sick **Feeling:** empathy	▪ Leo Lion's friends are coming to see him. Why are they coming to see him? ▪ At the end of the story, Leo Lion was happy. Why was Leo happy? ▪ In this story, Leo Lion's friends did nice things for him. Why should you do nice things for your friends?
Review	9	*Jungle Friends Go to the Park* 	soar ill ruin comfort reckless imagine	comforting a sick friend; field trips; exploration	  
3	10	*Ellie Gets Stuck* 	leap pause **Concept Word:** between	helping; working and playing together; playing tag **Feeling:** worry	▪ The Jungle Friends are playing tag. What game do you like to play? ▪ The friends all tried to help Ellie Elephant. Why did they help Ellie? ▪ Do you think Ellie Elephant will try to jump between the trees again?
	11	*A New Jungle Friend* 	speedy wise **Concept Word:** around	appreciating differences; everyone is unique **Feeling:** pride	▪ Tanisha Toucan wishes she was different. Why does she wish she was different? ▪ What did the Jungle Friends learn from the snake? ▪ The Jungle Friends can each do something special. What is something special that you can do?
	12	*Marquez's Backwards Day* 	ridiculous tumble **Concept Words:** day, night	playing together; opposites **Feeling:** silliness	▪ Leo Lion told Marquez Monkey to turn around. Why did he tell Marquez that? ▪ The Jungle Friends thought Marquez Monkey was silly. Why did they think he was silly? ▪ Do you think Marquez Monkey will have another backwards day?
Review	13	*Jungle Friends Swing Through the Vines* 	wise pause leap speedy ridiculous tumble	planning and competing in a race; having fun versus winning **Feeling:** excitement	  

√ = Tested Skills

Forest Friends

Week 14

Meet the Forest Friends

Introduce the book series and characters.

Pablo Porcupine

Fae Fox

Bobby Bear

Suki Squirrel

Unit	Week	Book	Vocabulary √	Topics	Comprehension Questions
4	15	*Pablo's Pricky Problem* 	terrified protect **Concept Words:** largest, smallest	first day of school; making friends with others who are different **Feeling:** fear	▪ Pablo Porcupine is sad. Why is Pablo sad? ▪ At the beginning of the story, the other animals in Pablo Porcupine's class were afraid of him. Why were they afraid of Pablo? ▪ Remember when Suki Squirrel asked Pablo Porcupine to play? Why did Suki ask Pablo to play?
	16	*Suki's Sleepover Surprise* 	agree disappointed **Concept Words:** first, last	sleepovers **Feelings:** disappoint-ment, sadness, surprise	▪ Suki Squirrel is excited. Why is Suki excited? ▪ Suki Squirrel's mom took her to the movies. Why did she take Suki to the movies? ▪ The Forest Friends watched cartoons and read a story at Suki's sleepover. What do you like to do with your friends?
	17	*Bobby's EmBEARassing Visit* 	kind accident **Concept Words:** tall, short	comforting a scared friend; going to the doctor **Feelings:** kindnesss, embarrassment	▪ Bobby Bear is scared. Why is Bobby scared? ▪ In this story, the friends went to the doctor with Bobby Bear. Why did they go with them? ▪ Do you think Bobby Bear will be scared the next time he goes to the doctor?
Review	18	*Suki Squirrel Goes Swimming* 	agree terrified grin kind accident protect disappointed	helping a scared friend; going swimming **Feeling:** fear	  
5	19	*Fae's Nose Knows* 	lost worried **Concept Words:** near, far	understanding others' feelings; getting lost **Feeling:** worry	▪ Fae's grandma is happy. Why is she happy? ▪ When the friends got to the den, Fae Fox told her grand-mother she was sorry. Why did Fae say she was sorry? ▪ Do you think the Forest Friends will visit Fae's grandma again?

√ = Tested Skills

Unit	Week	Book	Vocabulary √	Topics	Comprehension Questions
5	20	*Snow Day for Fae* 	complete frosty **Concept Words:** bottom, top	playing together; snow days; building snow figures; sledding **Feelings:** accomplishment, disappointment	▪ School is closed, so Fae Fox is going to play outside. What do you like to do when school is closed? ▪ At the beginning of the story, Fae's friends were waiting at her house. Why were her friends waiting for her? ▪ The next time it snows, do you think the Forest Friends will sled down the big hill again?
	21	*Where Is Bobby Bear?* 	exhausted search **Concept Words:** winter, spring	missing a friend; hibernation **Feelings:** exhaustion, worry	▪ Pablo, Fae, and Suki are looking everywhere for Bobby Bear. Why are they looking for Bobby? ▪ What did the Forest Friends learn from the bird? ▪ At the end of the story, the friends were happy. Why were the friends happy?
Review	22	*Pablo Packs a Picnic* 	complete search lost worried frosty exhausted	eating together; going on a picnic; getting lost **Feelings:** excitement, worry, exhaustion	  
6	23	*Pablo's Map Matters* 	thrilled ignore **Concept Words:** quiet, loud	listening; going to a carnival; using a map **Feeling:** thrill	▪ Pablo Porcupine brought a map with him. Why did Pablo bring a map? ▪ At the end of the story, the friends finally listened to Pablo Porcupine. Why should you listen to your friends? ▪ Do you think Pablo Porcupine's friends will listen to him the next time they play together?
	24	*Fae's Smelly Situation* 	horrible fail **Concept Words:** in, out	getting sprayed by a skunk **Feelings:** sadness, fear	▪ Fae Fox is sad. Why is Fae sad? ▪ In this story, the friends tried to help Fae Fox get clean. Why did they help Fae? ▪ Remember, Fae's friends tried to help her. What can you do to help your friends?
	25	*Suki's Selfish Saturday* 	selfish enjoy **Concept Words:** new, old	sharing **Feeling:** selfishness	▪ Suki Squirrel does not want to share her game. Why doesn't Suki want to share her game? ▪ At the end of the story, the friends shared their toys with each other. Why should you share with your friends? ▪ The next time Suki's friends come to her tree, do you think she will share with them?
Review	26	*Forest Friends Go to the Library* 	thrilled enjoy ignore horrible selfish fail	sharing; helping; going to the library **Feelings:** excitement, selfishness	  

√ = Tested Skills

The Listening Center

What Is the Listening Center?

The *Story Friends* intervention curriculum is delivered at the Listening Center. The Listening Center is an area in your classroom where children listen to the stories and instruction based on those stories. At small group listening centers, typically for three children, each child has a storybook and follows along as a narrator reads stories and delivers vocabulary and comprehension lessons. During each 10- to 15-minute session, children listen to a story and interact with the storybook, engage in vocabulary activities, and answer questions that develop comprehension skills. A facilitator—a teacher or another adult such as an assistant teacher, paraprofessional, or parent—monitors and guides children at the Listening Center.

- *Who is at the Listening Center?*
  - Two or three children
  - One facilitator
- *How long is each listening session?*
  - 10–15 minutes
- *What happens at the Listening Center?*
  - Each child has a storybook and headphones.
  - Children listen to stories and lessons.
  - Children respond to interactive prompts.
  - The facilitator monitors and guides children.
  - The facilitator may or may not also have a storybook.

Setting Up the Listening Center

Select a quiet spot for the Listening Center, such as a designated reading area. Keeping the Listening Center time consistent each day helps children build a routine. The Listening Center works best when scheduled during times that children already work in small groups:

- **Center time**
- **Small group time**
- **Free-choice time**

Running the Listening Center

To ensure that learning outcomes are met as children participate in the *Story Friends* program, it is important to set up the Listening Center to run smoothly. Before you begin each Listening Center session, ensure that:

- Children are in their assigned seats.
- Each child has the correct storybook.
- Each child has headphones on and is ready to begin listening.
- Children have enough space to turn the pages of their storybooks.
- The facilitator is seated close enough to children to help them turn pages.

During the Listening Center session, the facilitator helps children follow along by responding to prompts with children. Refer to the Listening Center strategies that follow for tips on participating in the lessons. In addition, ensure that:

- The correct audio is playing.
- Children are always on the correct page.
- Children respond to all questions.
- Children are engaged and participate throughout the entire session.

After the Listening Center session, use the Attendance Logs on pages 108–113 of this Teacher Guide to track that children listen to each storybook three times in a week. In the partial sample that follows, note that for the three listens of *Ellie's First Day,* Henry listened the first two days of the week for the first two listens (10/22 and 10/23). However, Henry was absent on the third day of the week (10/24), so the teacher recorded that Henry's third listen occurred on the fourth day of the week in a make-up session (10/25).

***Jungle Friends* Unit 1 Attendance Log**

Directions: Record the date each time children listen to a story.

Unit 1	Week 1 Meet the Jungle Friends			Week 2 Ellie's First Day			
Child	Listen 1	Listen 2	Listen 3	Listen 1	Listen 2	Listen 3	Listen
Henry	10/15	10/16	10/17	10/22	10/23	10/25	
Amar'e	10/15	10/16	10/17	10/22	10/23	10/24	
Supriya	10/15	10/16	10/17	10/22	10/23	10/24	

The Listening Center Quick Reference Guide

You might want to use *The Listening Center Quick Reference Guide* on page 114 of this Teacher Guide to keep helpful reminders for running the Listening Center.

Listening Center

Quick Reference Guide

Before each Listening Center session:

☑ Children are in their assigned seats.

☑ Each child has the correct storybook.

☑ Each child has headphones on and is ready to begin listening.

☑ Children have enough space to turn pages.

☑ I am close enough to help children turn pages.

During each Listening Center session:

☑ The correct audio is playing.

☑ Children are on the correct page.

☑ Children are responding to questions.

☑ Children are engaged and participating.

After each Listening Center session:

☑ I completed the Attendance Log.

At the end of each 5-day period:

☑ Each child listened to the storybook three times.

☑ The next storybooks are ready and the audio is cued up.

☑ The audio equipment is functioning properly.

17

The Listening Center Quick Reference Guide, p. 114

Starting the Program

Meet the Jungle Friends and *Meet the Forest Friends* are the introductory storybooks in each book series of *Story Friends.* These storybooks introduce children to the recurring characters of each series. With *Meet the Jungle Friends,* children can practice listening, wearing their headphones, and turning pages, and you can teach them the following expectations for the Listening Center. You can review the expectations when children begin the second storybook series, *Meet the Forest Friends.*

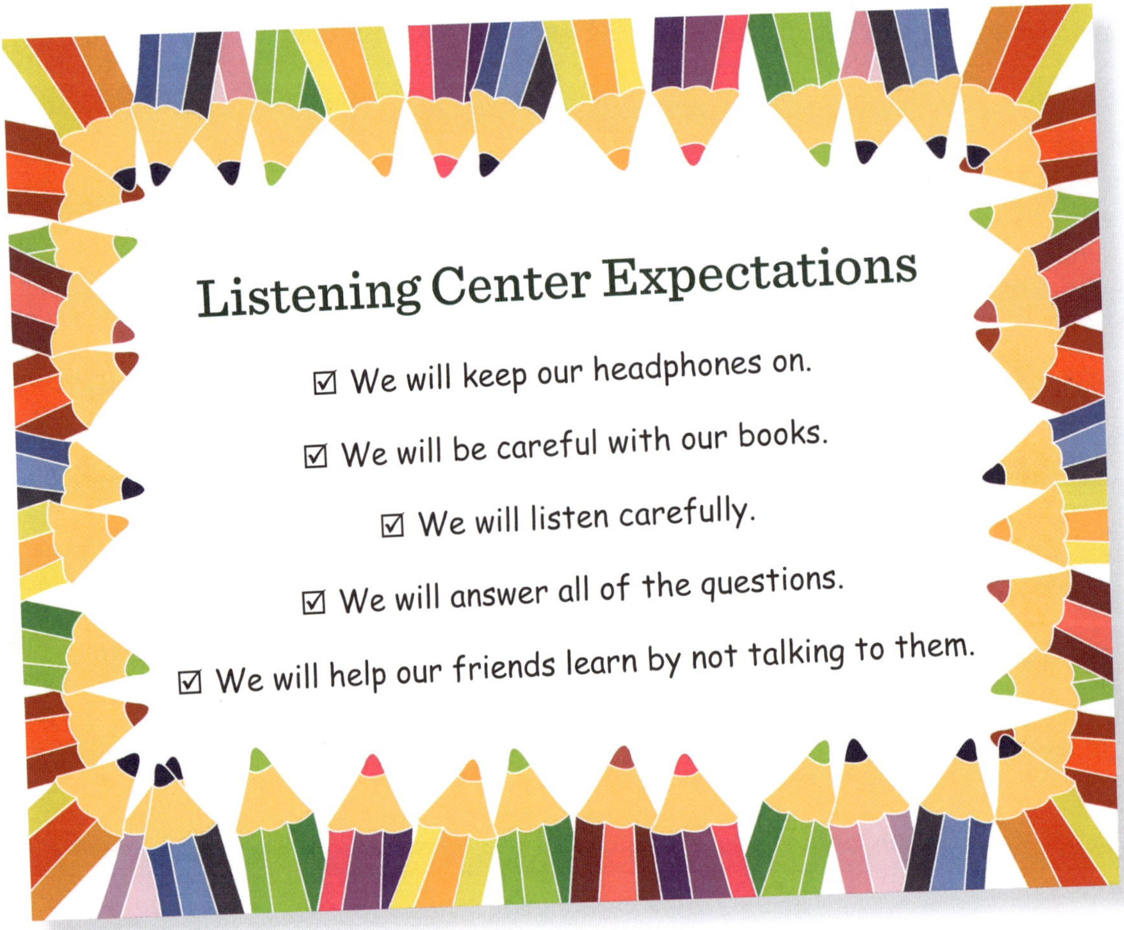

Listening Center Strategies

Children enjoy coming to the Listening Center to participate in the activities. The following strategies will encourage optimal student engagement and interaction.

- The facilitator draws the child's attention to the lesson. For example, when the narrator, Wanda the Word Wolf, begins to ask a question, the facilitator might say, "Oooh, listen!"
- The facilitator redirects the child's attention using nonverbal communication. Because children need to listen to the audio recording for the instruction, it is helpful to minimize verbal redirection. For example, instead of saying, "Shh, listen," it is more effective to use nonverbal communication, such as tapping your headphones or moving your index finger to your lips.
- The facilitator encourages children to participate by praising them using nonverbal communication. For example, "clapping" silently or smiling and nodding when children respond encourages children to continue to participate.
- The facilitator responds to the lesson prompts with children. Especially at the beginning of the program, children may not be accustomed to responding to an audio recording. When the facilitator responds along with children, they become more comfortable responding. For example, when the narrator asks children to "stretch their arms wide," the facilitator does this as well to model an appropriate response.

Participating in Lessons

In addition to responding to lesson prompts by gesturing, facilitators also can participate in lessons by responding verbally to prompts. See the following examples:

Audio Script: Enormous. Say enormous. Enormous means really big. What word means really big?
(The facilitator waits a few seconds to allow children to respond.)

Facilitator: ... Enormous!

Audio Script: Can you tell me some things that are enormous?
(The facilitator waits a few seconds to allow children to respond.)

Facilitator: ... A big truck!

Audio Script: I'm thinking of a school bus! A mountain! Or a building! Those are things that are really big. Tell me, what does *enormous* mean?
(The facilitator waits a few seconds to allow children to respond.)

Facilitator: ... Really big!

Story Friends Lessons: Audio Script

Wanda the Word Wolf narrates the *Story Friends* series. Her image on storybook pages and this script correspond to embedded vocabulary and comprehension lessons.

STORY FRIENDS

Jungle Friends

Unit 1, Week 1

Meet the Jungle Friends

Aroo, aroo. Hello. Welcome to the Listening Center. Do you have your book? **PAUSE.** Make sure it is closed, and do not open it until I tell you to. Look at the front cover of your book. Do you see a picture of animals on the cover? **PAUSE.** Yes! Do you see some words there at the top? **PAUSE.** This is the name of the book. The name of a book is called the title. Now, put your finger under the first word of the title. Follow the arrow under the words as we read the title of the book together. It says, *Meet the Jungle Friends.*

Go ahead and open your book now.

Hello again! My name is Wanda the Word Wolf. Do you see me? I have pointy ears and a fluffy tail. What's your name? **PAUSE.** Great! It's nice to meet you.

Every time you come to the Listening Center, you will get a book to read with me. And when you hear me say *Aroo, aroo,* it means it is time for you to listen and answer some questions.

Let's practice.

Aroo, aroo. Did you hear me say *Aroo, aroo*? **PAUSE.** Let's answer a question. Are you ready? **PAUSE.** Okay! Here's one: How old are you? **PAUSE.** Great job! Now point to my nose. What color is my nose? **PAUSE.** Black! That's right!

In this book, we are going to meet some more new friends. When you hear this sound it means you can go ahead and turn the page. Let's turn the page now.

Turn the page.

Do you see the picture of the jungle? **PAUSE.** A jungle is a hot, wet place with lots of trees, plants, and animals. Today you will meet four animals called the Jungle Friends! First is Leo Lion. He is roaring. Point to Leo Lion. **PAUSE.** Next is Ellie Elephant. She is holding a flag. Point to Ellie Elephant. **PAUSE.** Tanisha Toucan is high up in the tree. Do you see her? Point to Tanisha Toucan. **PAUSE.** Last is Marquez Monkey. He is hanging upside down in a tree. Point to Marquez Monkey. **PAUSE.**

Great listening! Let's start our story now.

Turn the page.

[p. 5]
The Jungle Friends are getting ready.
They cannot wait!
It's the first day of school,
and they don't want to be late.

Turn the page.

[p. 6]
Ellie Elephant is running out the door.
She does not want to be late.
"Hooray!" she says. "It's time for school.
I cannot wait!"

Aroo, aroo. Did you hear me say *Aroo, aroo*? **PAUSE.** Let's answer a question. Are you ready? **PAUSE.** Ellie Elephant is leaving for school. Now lift the brown bag. **PAUSE.** What is Ellie taking for lunch? **PAUSE.** Peanuts and jelly! Nice work!

Turn the page.

[p. 9]
Marquez Monkey is leaving his house, too.
He does not want to be late.
"Yeah!" he says. "It's time for school.
I cannot wait!"

Aroo, aroo. Marquez needs to get his backpack. Lift the backpack to see what Marquez will need for school. **PAUSE.** I see some crayons. Say crayons. **PAUSE.** I see a book. Say book. **PAUSE.** Great job!

Turn the page.

[p. 11]
Leo Lion is saying goodbye to his mom.
He does not want to be late.
"Woohoo!" he says. "It's time for school.
I cannot wait!"

Aroo, aroo. Leo Lion is blowing a kiss to his mom as he leaves for school. Pretend you are blowing a kiss to someone. **PAUSE.** That's nice!

Turn the page.

[p. 13]
Tanisha Toucan is flying to school.
She does not want to be late.
"Yippee!" she says. "It's time for school.
I cannot wait!"

Aroo, aroo. Lift the flap to see what Tanisha will do at the school playground. **PAUSE.** Play on the slide! What do you like to do at the playground? **PAUSE.** I like to swing.

Turn the page.

[p. 15]
Marquez, Tanisha, Ellie, and Leo
found their way.
They are so excited for
their first school day!

Aroo, aroo. The Jungle Friends made it to their classroom. They look happy. Why are the Jungle Friends happy? **PAUSE.** Because it's their first day of school!

You did a great job answering questions today! Now, can you find me, Wanda the Word Wolf, on this page? **PAUSE.** Remember, every time you come to the listening center, you will get a book to read with me. And when you hear me say, *Aroo, aroo,* it means it is time for you to listen and answer some questions.

I had a lot of fun with you in the Listening Center today! Thank you for coming! Raise your hand so your teacher knows you are finished. See you tomorrow!

Unit 1, Week 2

Ellie's First Day

Vocabulary: enormous, different
Concept Words: high, low

Aroo, aroo. Hello again! Welcome to the listening center. It's me, Wanda the Word Wolf. Remember, when you hear me say *Aroo, aroo,* it means it is time for you to answer some questions.

Do you have your book? **PAUSE.** Make sure it is closed, and do not open it until I tell you to. Look at the front cover of your book. Do you see a picture of Ellie Elephant on the cover? **PAUSE.** Yes! Now put your finger under the first word of the title. Follow the arrow under the words as we read the title of the book together. It says, *Ellie's First Day.*

Go ahead and open your book now.

Turn the page.

[p. 2]
The first day of school
was a big day for Ellie.
Her mom packed a lunch
full of peanuts and jelly.

Turn the page.

[p. 4]
Ellie grabbed her bags
and ran straight outside.
How exciting—
her very first school bus ride!

Aroo, aroo. Ellie Elephant is excited! Why is Ellie excited? **PAUSE.** Ellie is excited because it is her first day of school! She gets to ride the school bus and meet her new teacher! That sounds fun!

Turn the page.

[p. 6]
Ellie was enormous,
so she had to squeeze in tight.
When she got on the bus,
it tilted to the right!

Aroo, aroo. Ellie is enormous! She is really big! Enormous. Say enormous. **PAUSE.** Enormous means really big. What word means really big? **PAUSE.** Enormous! Great job! Let's see. Can you tell me some things that are enormous? **PAUSE.** I'm thinking of a school bus! A mountain! Or a building! Those are things that are really big. Now, pretend you are going to give Ellie a hug. Remember, she is enormous, so make your arms really big! Whew! Tell me, what does enormous mean? **PAUSE.** Really big! That's right!

Turn the page.

[p. 9]
All the kids started giggling,
HA HA, HE HE!
"Oh, no!" thought Ellie.
"They are laughing at me!"

Turn the page.

[p. 10]
Ellie got to class
and sat down in a chair.
She was so big that it broke.
There were pieces everywhere!

Turn the page.

[p. 13]
All the kids started giggling,
HA HA, HE HE!
"Oh, no!" thought Ellie.
"They are laughing at me!"

Turn the page.

[p. 15]
On the playground, Ellie thought
that the see-saw looked fun.
Nobody could lift her,
but she lifted everyone.

Turn the page.

[p. 16]
All the kids started giggling,
HA HA, HE HE!
"Oh, no!" thought Ellie.
"They are laughing at me!"

Turn the page.

[p. 19]
At lunchtime Ellie took out her food.
Then she thought,
"My lunch is different
from what the other kids brought."

Aroo, aroo. Ellie's lunch is different. Her lunch is not the same. Different. Say different. **PAUSE.** Different means not the same. What word means not the same? **PAUSE.** Different! Great job! Let's see. I bet you are wearing different shoes than your friends. Look and see. Are your shoes the same as your friends' shoes? **PAUSE.** No. They are probably different. Look at the dots! Do they look the same? **PAUSE.** No, one is different. Put your finger on the one that is different. Did you put your finger on the one that is green? **PAUSE.** Good job! The green one is different. It is not the same as the others. Tell me, what does different mean? **PAUSE.** Not the same! That's right!

Turn the page.

[p. 21]
The kids said,
"Why do you have all those peanuts, Ellie?
You're supposed to have
peanut butter and jelly!"

Turn the page.

[p. 22]
All the kids started giggling,
HA HA, HE HE!
"Oh, no!" thought Ellie.
"They are laughing at me!"

Turn the page.

[p. 24]
After lunch all the kids
were playing kickball.
Leo Lion was the best
player of them all.

Turn the page.

[p. 26]
He kicked the ball into a tree.
It got stuck up high.
Ellie said, "I can help,
if you will let me try."

Turn the page.

[p. 29]
Ellie leaned against the tree
until it bent down low.
"You can reach it now!" she said.
"Come get the ball, Leo."

Aroo, aroo. Oh my goodness! The ball was stuck high in the tree! High. Say high. **PAUSE.** Put your hand way up high in the air! Then Ellie bent the tree way down low. Low. Say low. **PAUSE.** Put your hand very low. Awesome job!

Turn the page.

[p. 30]
Leo shouted, "Thank you, Ellie!
You're so strong! Woohoo!"
"You did it," Marquez Monkey cried.
"You're smart and helpful, too!

Turn the page.

[p. 32]
"We're sorry we laughed at you,"
Tanisha Toucan said.
"From now on, we should all
be best friends instead!"

Turn the page.

[p. 34]
That night Ellie told her mom
all about her day,
about the new friends she made,
and the games that they would play!

Aroo, aroo. Ellie had an exciting day! Hmm. I have some questions for you. The other kids laughed at Ellie Elephant. Why did they laugh at Ellie? **PAUSE.** Because she was new! Ellie broke her chair, and no one could lift her on the see-saw. The other kids didn't know her yet, so they laughed at her.

At the end of the story, Ellie Elephant was happy. Why was Ellie happy? **PAUSE.** Because she made some new friends! I bet she felt happy to have new friends.

Turn the page.

Let's talk about the words we learned!

Look at the picture of the dump truck. It is really big! The dump truck is enormous. Say enormous. **PAUSE.** Tell me, what does enormous mean? **PAUSE.** Really big! Great job!

Now look at the picture of Ellie and the other Jungle Friends. The friends do not look the same. They look different. Say different. **PAUSE.** Tell me, what does different mean? **PAUSE.** Not the same! That's right!

Turn the page.

Point to the balloon in the sky. Is the balloon high or low? **PAUSE.** High! Great job!

Now point to the ball on the ground. Is the ball high or low? **PAUSE.** Low! Great thinking!

I had a lot of fun with you in the listening center today! Thank you for coming! Raise your hand so your teacher knows you are finished. See you tomorrow!

Unit 1, Week 3

Leo's Brave Face

Vocabulary: brave, grin
Concept Word: all

Aroo, aroo. Hello again! Welcome to the Listening Center. It's me, Wanda the Word Wolf. Remember, when you hear me say *Aroo, aroo,* it means it is time for you to answer some questions.

Do you have your book? **PAUSE.** Make sure it is closed, and do not open it until I tell you to. Look at the front cover of your book. Do you see a picture of Leo Lion on the cover? **PAUSE.** Yes! Now put your finger under the first word of the title. Follow the arrow under the words as we read the title of the book together. It says, *Leo's Brave Face.*

Go ahead and open your book now.

Turn the page.

[p. 2]
One night before bedtime,
Leo Lion's mother said,
"You have a dentist visit tomorrow.
Brush your teeth, and go to bed."

Turn the page.

[p. 4]
Leo Lion was afraid,
but he knew
that he had to be brave
because that's what lions do!

Aroo, aroo. Leo Lion is afraid. Why is he afraid? **PAUSE.** Because he is going to the dentist. Leo has never been to the dentist before. It can be scary to do new things.

Turn the page.

[p. 6]
The next morning, Leo woke up
and brushed his teeth once more.
Then he put on his brave face
and walked out the door.

Turn the page.

[p. 9]
On the way to the dentist,
he saw his friends playing a game.
Marquez said, "Hey, Leo!
We are so glad that you came!"

Turn the page.

[p. 10]
But Leo had to tell his friends
that he could not stay.
He had a dentist visit
and must be on his way.

Turn the page.

[p. 12]
Ellie asked,
"Do you want us to come along?"
Leo said, "No. Don't worry.
I'll be brave and strong."

Aroo, aroo. Leo will be brave! He won't be scared of the dentist. Brave. Say brave. **PAUSE.** Brave means not scared. What word means not scared? **PAUSE.** Brave! Let's think of a time when you are brave. Sometimes, I'm scared to go down the big slide at the playground. I'm scared to go really fast. I have to be very brave. Does that happen to you, too? **PAUSE.** Look at Leo. He doesn't look scared. He is brave. Tell Leo, "Be brave!" **PAUSE.** Tell me, what does brave mean? **PAUSE.** Not scared! That's right.

Turn the page.

[p. 15]
When Leo arrived at the dentist,
he waited for them to call his name.
He could choose to read a book,
play with toys, or play a game.

Turn the page.

[p. 16]
So Leo opened up a book
and read for a while.
Soon the dentist arrived.
He was a crocodile!

Turn the page.

[p. 18]
In the dentist's office,
there was a big, comfy chair.
Leo sat and looked around.
He tried not to be scared.

Turn the page.

[p. 21]
The dentist said,
"Now I need to take a look inside.
So tilt back your head
and open up wide."

Turn the page.

[p. 22]
"You have such big teeth," said the dentist.
"Now let's make them clean.
I will brush the front and back,
and I will floss in between."

Turn the page.

[p. 24]
Leo kept his mouth open
until the dentist was all done.
Then the dentist showed him toothbrushes
and said he could pick one.

Aroo, aroo. Look at all those toothbrushes! All. Say all. **PAUSE.** Is the dentist going to give Leo all those toothbrushes? **PAUSE.** No. He will get just one. Let's see. Can you show me all your fingers? **PAUSE.** I see all of them. Great job!

Turn the page.

[p. 26]
"And remember," said the dentist,
"you must brush every night.
It will keep those big teeth of yours
healthy and bright."

Turn the page.

[p. 29]
When Leo walked in his door,
he started to grin.
He told his mom he couldn't wait
to visit the dentist again.

Aroo, aroo. Look at Leo. He is grinning. He had fun at the dentist, so he is smiling! Grin. Say grin. **PAUSE.** Grin means to smile. Tell me what word means to smile? **PAUSE.** Grin. Great job! Now *you* grin. Smile and say, "Cheese!" **PAUSE.** That's fun! Now, open the doors. **PAUSE.** This little boy is grinning, too. Tell me, what does grin mean? **PAUSE.** To smile. Great job!

♫ Turn the page.

[p. 30]
And later that night
before Leo went to bed,
he made sure to brush his teeth
just like the dentist said.

Aroo, aroo. What a great story! Leo went to the dentist. Hmm. I have some questions for you.

What did Leo Lion learn from the dentist? **PAUSE.** Leo learned to keep his teeth clean. Remember? The dentist told him to brush his teeth every night.

Do you think Leo Lion will brush his teeth every night? **PAUSE.** Yes, I think so! He will brush his teeth, because the dentist said that will keep them healthy.

♫ Turn the page.

Let's talk about the words we learned! Look at the little girl getting on the bus. She is riding the school bus for the first time. She is not scared. She is brave. Say brave. **PAUSE.** Tell me, what does brave mean? **PAUSE.** Not scared. Great job!

Look at the girls taking a picture. They are smiling for the camera! They are grinning! Say grin. **PAUSE.** Tell me, what does grin mean? **PAUSE.** To smile. All right!

♫ Turn the page.

Look at the picture of the Jungle Friends! Point to all of them. I see Leo and Tanisha and Marquez and Ellie. Do you see Leo by himself or do you see all of the Jungle Friends? **PAUSE.** All of them. Great job!

I had a lot of fun with you in the Listening Center today! Thank you for coming! Raise your hand so your teacher knows you are finished. See you tomorrow!

Unit 1, Week 4

Jungle Friends Go to the Beach

Vocabulary: gorgeous, soaked
Concept Words: many, few

Aroo, aroo. Hello again! Welcome to the Listening Center. It's me, Wanda the Word Wolf. Remember, when you hear me say *Aroo, aroo,* it means it is time for you to answer some questions.

Do you have your book? **PAUSE.** Make sure it is closed, and do not open it until I tell you to. Look at the front cover of your book. Do you see a picture of Leo Lion on the cover? **PAUSE.** Yes! Now, put your finger under the first word of the title. Follow the arrow under the words as we read the title of the book together. It says, *Jungle Friends Go to the Beach.*

♫ Go ahead and open your book now.

♫ Turn the page.

[p. 2]
One morning, the
Jungle Friends thought it
would be fun to take a trip to the
beach and play in the sun.

♫ Turn the page.

[p. 4]
Tanisha Toucan brought a bucket.
Marquez Monkey brought a net.
Ellie Elephant brought her surfboard.
Leo brought towels for when they got wet.

Turn the page.

[p. 7]
The friends wanted to have fun
with each other all day.
But no one could decide
what they wanted to play.

Turn the page.

[p. 9]
Leo thought it would be nice
to lie under the sun.
But Ellie thought that surfing
would be the most fun.

Turn the page.

[p. 10]
Marquez would look for gorgeous seashells.
He hoped to find them all.
Tanisha decided to build a sandcastle.
She would make it big and tall.

Aroo, aroo. Marquez wants to find seashells. The seashells are gorgeous. They are pretty! Gorgeous. Say gorgeous. **PAUSE.** Gorgeous means pretty. Tell me, what word means pretty? **PAUSE.** Gorgeous. That's right! Tell me some things that you think are gorgeous. **PAUSE.** I think flowers, butterflies, and sparkly rings are gorgeous! They are pretty. Now, open the seashell to see something else gorgeous. **PAUSE.** Wow! What a pretty sticker! It is gorgeous. Tell me, what does gorgeous mean? **PAUSE.** Pretty. Great thinking!

Turn the page.

[p. 12]
So Leo lay on the beach
and wore his new shades.
He enjoyed the warm breeze
and a glass of cool lemonade.

Turn the page.

[p. 14]
Marquez found many
pretty seashells in the sand.
He collected a few in his net,
just like he had planned.

Aroo, aroo. Marquez found many seashells in the sand! Many. Say many. **PAUSE.** Can you help Marquez find seashells? Look under the rock. **PAUSE.** There are only a few seashells there. Few. Say few. **PAUSE.** Great work!

Turn the page.

[p. 17]
Tanisha used her bucket
to stack up sand very tall.
She built a huge sandcastle,
and hoped it would not fall.

Aroo, aroo. Tanisha Toucan is happy. Why is Tanisha happy? **PAUSE.** Because she built a huge sandcastle. It is fun to play in the sand.

Turn the page.

[p. 19]
Ellie rode the waves
on her striped surfboard.
She felt like she was flying
as up and down she soared.

Turn the page.

[p. 21]
But then she teetered and tottered,
and with a big crash,
Ellie fell into the water
and made a huge SPLASH!

Turn the page.

[p. 22]
The wave washed away
the shells Marquez had found!
And it knocked Tanisha's sandcastle
all over the ground!

Turn the page.

[p. 24]
All the friends got soaked,
but Leo had good news.
He had brought towels
for everyone to use!

Aroo, aroo. The Jungle Friends are soaked! They are really wet! Soaked. Say soaked. **PAUSE.** Soaked means really wet. Tell me, what word means really wet? **PAUSE.** Soaked! That's right! When you get out of the bathtub or the swimming pool, are you soaked? **PAUSE.** I bet you are really wet. Look at the picture of Leo Lion. See all the water on him? He is really wet! He is soaked! Pretend you are soaked, too. Grab a towel and rub your body until you're dry. **PAUSE.** That feels better! Tell me, what does soaked mean? **PAUSE.** Really wet. Great work!

Turn the page.

[p. 27]
Then Marquez decided
they should play something together.
"Tanisha, we'll all help you build
the best sandcastle ever!"

Turn the page.

[p. 28]
The Jungle Friends found out
that working together was more fun!
And they played games with each other
until the day was done.

Aroo, aroo. Wow! The Jungle Friends had a great time playing at the beach. Hmm. I have some questions for you. At the end of the story, the Jungle Friends worked together. Why should you work together with your friends? **PAUSE.** Because it is more fun to work together! If you work with your friends, it is easy to get something done. The Jungle Friends liked working together better than playing alone.

Do you think the Jungle Friends will go to the beach again? **PAUSE.** Yes, I think so! They had a great time playing at the beach. Ellie went surfing, and Marquez found shells. They will probably want to go back.

Turn the page.

Let's talk about the words we learned! Look at the picture of the fireflies! When fireflies light up, they are pretty. Fireflies are gorgeous! Say gorgeous. **PAUSE.** Tell me, what does gorgeous mean? **PAUSE.** Pretty. That's right!

Look at the picture of the rain. If you play in the rain, you might get really wet! You might get soaked. Say soaked. **PAUSE.** Tell me, what does soaked mean? **PAUSE.** Really wet! Great thinking!

Turn the page.

Look! Ellie is eating her lunch. Point to the peanuts. Does she have a few peanuts or many peanuts? **PAUSE.** Many. That's right!

Now lift the flap. Point to her peanuts now. Does she have a few or many? **PAUSE.** Few. Great work!

I had a lot of fun with you in the Listening Center today! Thank you for coming! Raise your hand so your teacher knows you are finished. See you tomorrow!

Unit 1 Review, Week 5

Jungle Friends Bake a Cake

Vocabulary Review: grin, different, enormous, gorgeous, brave, soaked

Aroo, aroo. Hello again! Welcome to the Listening Center. It's me, Wanda the Word Wolf. Remember, when you hear me say *Aroo, aroo,* it means it is time for you to answer some questions.

Do you have your book? **PAUSE.** Make sure it is closed, and do not open it until I tell you to. Look at the front cover of your book. Do you see a picture of Marquez Monkey on the cover? **PAUSE.** Yes! Now put your finger under the first word of the title. Follow the arrow under the words as we read the title of the book together. It says, *Jungle Friends Bake a Cake.*

Go ahead and open your book now.

Turn the page.

[p. 2]
One morning at school,
the Jungle Friends were playing games.
"I sure am hungry," Leo Lion said.

Turn the page.

[p. 4]
"Why don't we bake a cake?"
asked the teacher, Ms. Hippo.
"If we bake a cake,
you will not be hungry anymore."

Turn the page.

[p. 7]
"Yippee!" said the Jungle Friends.
Baking a cake would be a lot of fun.
The friends were so happy, they grinned.

Aroo, aroo. Look at the friends smiling. They are grinning! Grin. Say grin. **PAUSE.** Grin means to smile. Tell me, what does grin mean? **PAUSE.** To smile. You got it!

Turn the page.

[p. 8]
The friends went into the kitchen to bake the cake.
Ms. Hippo gave the friends a big bowl
and some spoons to get them started.

Turn the page.

[p. 10]
First, Ellie Elephant put some eggs into the bowl.
Next, Leo Lion added sugar.
Then, Tanisha Toucan poured in some chocolate.
Each friend put something different into the bowl.

Aroo, aroo. Each friend is holding something different. The eggs, sugar, and chocolate are not the same. Different. Say different. **PAUSE.** Different means not the same. Tell me, what does different mean? **PAUSE.** Not the same. That's right!

Turn the page.

[p. 13]
After Marquez Monkey mixed
the ingredients together,
the friends poured the cake mix into a pan.
"I can't wait to eat this cake," said Tanisha happily.

Turn the page.

[p. 14]
Ms. Hippo took the pan from the friends
and placed it into the oven.
Soon, the cake started to smell yummy,
and all of the friends got excited.

Turn the page.

[p. 16]
When the cake came out of the oven,
the friends could not believe how big it was.
The cake was enormous!

Aroo, aroo. Look at the cake. It is really big. It is enormous! Say enormous. **PAUSE.** Enormous means really big. Tell me, what does enormous mean? **PAUSE.** Really big. Nice thinking!

Turn the page.

[p. 19]
"Let's decorate the cake," yelled Ellie.
"I have some icing and sprinkles!"
The friends began to put frosting
all over the huge cake.

Turn the page.

[p. 20]
Next, Marquez Monkey began to
put sprinkles on the cake.
"Wow," said Leo Lion.
"The cake is so pretty. It looks gorgeous!"

Aroo, aroo. Look at the pretty cake! The cake is gorgeous. Say gorgeous. **PAUSE.** Gorgeous means pretty. Tell me, what does gorgeous mean? **PAUSE.** Pretty. Good job!

Turn the page.

[p. 22]
Ms. Hippo told the friends,
"I think it just needs a cherry on top,
and then the cake will be all done!"
But the cake was so enormous,
the friends could not reach the top.

Turn the page.

[p. 24]
"I know," said Ellie Elephant.
"Stand on me, and then we will
reach the top together!"
So the Jungle Friends all climbed on top of Ellie.

Turn the page.

[p. 26]
Marquez Monkey decided to climb to the very top
to put the cherry on the cake.
He climbed way up high
because he was very brave.

Aroo, aroo. Look how high Marquez climbed! He is not scared. He's brave! Say brave. **PAUSE.** Brave means not scared. Tell me, what does brave mean? **PAUSE.** Not scared. That's right!

Turn the page.

[p. 29]
"Woohoo!" cheered the Jungle Friends!
"The cake is all done!"
The friends decided it was time
to eat a piece of cake.

Turn the page.

[p. 30]
First, Ms. Hippo poured each friend a cup of juice.
Leo wasn't looking where he was going,
and he bumped into Tanisha's cup.

Turn the page.

[p. 32]
Tanisha's juice went everywhere!
The juice got all over Leo, so he was dripping wet.
Leo was soaked!

Aroo, aroo. Oh, no! Leo Lion is really wet. He is soaked. Say soaked. **PAUSE.** Soaked means really wet. Tell me, what does soaked mean? **PAUSE.** Really wet. Nice job!

Turn the page.

[p. 34]
"Don't worry," said Ms. Hippo.
"Here's your cake! It is very tasty!"

Turn the page.

[p. 36]
The friends ate their cake.
It was so good,
they quickly forgot about the spilled juice.
What a fun day!

I had a lot of fun with you in the Listening Center today! Thank you for coming! Raise your hand so your teacher knows you are finished. See you tomorrow!

Unit 2, Week 6

Marquez Monkeys Around

Vocabulary: reckless, ruin
Concept Words: up, down

Aroo, aroo. Hello again. Welcome to the Listening Center. It's me, Wanda the Word

Wolf. Do you have your book? **PAUSE.** Do you see a picture of Marquez Monkey on the cover? **PAUSE.** Yes! Now put your finger under the first word of the title. Follow the arrow under the words as we read the title of the book together. It says, *Marquez Monkeys Around.*

Go ahead and open your book.

Turn the page.

[p. 2]
Marquez Monkey spent the day
building a tree house with his dad.
It was the best tree house
any monkey ever had.

Aroo, aroo. Look! Marquez is climbing up the ladder to help his dad. Up. Say up. **PAUSE.** I wonder when they will climb down. Down. Say down. **PAUSE.** Now lift the flap. **PAUSE.** See the slide? Climb your fingers up the ladder. Up, up, up! Now slide down! That was fun!

Turn the page.

[p. 5]
The next morning, the friends met
in the jungle to play.
But Marquez felt like swinging
around that day.

Turn the page.

[p. 6]
Ellie, Tanisha, and Leo
played in a group of three
while Marquez swung wildly
from tree to tree.

Turn the page.

[p. 8]
The friends worked on a puzzle.
They were almost done.
But Marquez kept swinging wildly,
and he messed up their fun.

Turn the page.

[p. 10]
Marquez was not being careful,
and he knocked a banana down.
The puzzle was a mess. The friends yelled,
"Marquez, stop monkeying around!"

Aroo, aroo. The friends are mad. Why are they mad? **PAUSE.** Because Marquez Monkey messed up their fun. The friends were almost done with their puzzle, and now it is in pieces. That's not fun!

Turn the page.

[p. 12]
"I have some marbles," said Ellie.
"We can play a game with them."
The game was really fun,
until Marquez swung by again.

Turn the page.

[p. 14]
Marquez was being reckless,
and he knocked two bananas down.
The marbles were a mess. The friends yelled,
"Marquez, stop monkeying around!"

Aroo, aroo. Marquez is swinging and knocking down bananas. He is reckless! He is not safe. Reckless. Say reckless. **PAUSE.** Reckless means not safe. Tell me, what word means not safe? **PAUSE.** Reckless. That's right! Hmm. Let's think about something that is reckless. If you run in the hallway at school, that is not safe. You might trip and fall. That is reckless. Now lift the flap. **PAUSE.** The Jungle Friends are climbing up the slide. They are not safe. They are reckless. Tell me, what does reckless mean? **PAUSE.** Not safe. Great thinking!

Turn the page.

[p. 17]
Then Leo said, "I know!
Let's paint a picture of a bee!"
The painting was almost done
when Marquez swung by wildly.

Turn the page.

[p. 18]
Marquez was not being careful,
and he knocked three bananas down.
The painting was a mess. The friends yelled,
"Marquez, stop monkeying around!"

Turn the page.

[p. 21]
But Marquez ignored them,
and he did not see
that he was heading right for
his own special tree.

Turn the page.

[p. 22]
It was the tree house he had built
with his dad yesterday.
He was getting very close.
He was not far away.

Turn the page.

[p. 24]
Marquez swung faster and faster,
and even faster still.
He was swinging and having fun
and not looking, until...

Turn the page.

[p. 26]
KABOOM!!!
The friends heard the crash
and came quickly to see
that Marquez had ruined
the tree house in his own tree.

Aroo, aroo. Oh, no! Marquez crashed into the tree and ruined his tree house. He messed it up! Ruin. Say ruin. **PAUSE.** Ruin means to mess up. Tell me, what word means to mess up? **PAUSE.** Ruin! Nice work. Marquez ruined a lot of things in this story. He messed up the puzzle, the marbles, Leo's painting, and now he ruined his tree house! Have you ever ruined something? **PAUSE.** Now, lift the flap.

PAUSE. Uh-oh! The dog ruined the teddy bear! He messed it up. Tell me, what does ruin mean? **PAUSE.** To mess up. You got it!

Turn the page.

[p. 29]
Now Marquez wished he had listened
to what his friends had said.
He decided to stop swinging
and play with them instead.

Turn the page.

[p. 31]
Marquez told them he was sorry,
and the friends all agreed.
They would fix the broken tree house
and help their friend in need!

Aroo, aroo. The friends helped Marquez fix his tree house. That's nice. Hmm. I have some questions for you. In this story, Marquez Monkey was not being careful. Why should you be careful? **PAUSE.** Because if you aren't careful, you might do something you didn't mean to do. Marquez messed up his friends' games and broke his tree house. You can hurt yourself or your friends if you aren't careful.

The next time Marquez Monkey goes to the jungle, do you think he will swing around wildly? **PAUSE.** No, I don't think so. I think he will play with his friends next time. His friends helped him fix his tree house, so he will want to play with them.

Turn the page.

Let's talk about the words we learned. Look at the picture of the boy standing on the monkey bars. He is not safe. He is reckless! Say reckless. **PAUSE.** Tell me, what does reckless mean? **PAUSE.** Not safe.

Look at the little boy with paint on his shirt. He messed up his shirt. He ruined it! Ruin. Say ruin. **PAUSE.** Tell me, what does ruin mean? **PAUSE.** To mess up. Good thinking!

Turn the page.

Look at Ellie Elephant. Is she up or down? **PAUSE.** Down! Good work!

Now look at the other friends. Are they up or down? **PAUSE.** Up. Awesome job!

I had a lot of fun with you in the Listening Center today! Thank you for coming! Raise your hand so your teacher knows you are finished. See you tomorrow!

Unit 2, Week 7

If Elephants Could Fly

Vocabulary: imagine, soar
Concept Words: soft, hard

Aroo, aroo. Hello again. Welcome to the Listening Center. It's me, Wanda the Word Wolf. Do you have your book? **PAUSE.** Do you see a picture of Ellie Elephant on the cover? **PAUSE.** Yes! Now put your finger under the first word of the title. Follow the arrow under the words as we read the title of the book together. It says, *If Elephants Could Fly.*

Go ahead and open your book now.

Turn the page.

[p. 2]
One hot afternoon, the Jungle Friends
took a nap beneath a tree.
But Ellie Elephant stayed awake.
She couldn't fall asleep.

Turn the page.

[p. 4]
Ellie gazed into the air
as a bird went flying by.
She began to wonder,
"What if elephants could fly?"

Turn the page.

[p. 6]
"I can imagine it!" thought Ellie,
and then she closed her eyes.
She pretended that she was
an elephant that flies!

Aroo, aroo. Ellie imagines that she can fly. She pretends. Imagine. Say imagine. **PAUSE.** Imagine means to pretend. Tell me, what word means to pretend? **PAUSE.** Imagine. That's right! Sometimes I like to imagine I am a superhero with special powers. It's fun to pretend! Now, close your eyes and imagine you can fly. Pretend you are way up in the sky! Tell me, what does imagine mean? **PAUSE.** To pretend. Great job!

Turn the page.

[p. 8]
Ellie imagined she could fly
high above the trees,
where she talked to little birds,
and enjoyed the cool breeze.

Turn the page.

[p. 10]
When Ellie got tired
from all the fluttering and soaring,
she rested in the clouds
until that got boring.

Aroo, aroo. Ellie is resting in the soft clouds! Soft. Say soft. **PAUSE.** Now lift the flap. **PAUSE.** It's a rock! A rock is hard. Say hard. **PAUSE.** Great job!

Turn the page.

[p. 12]
Then Ellie waved at her little brother
from way up in the sky.
He was so surprised
to see an elephant fly!

Aroo, aroo. Ellie Elephant's little brother is surprised. Why is he surprised? **PAUSE.** Because Ellie is flying! I bet he's never seen a flying elephant before. That would surprise me, too.

Turn the page.

[p. 15]
Ellie also waved at a pilot
in an airplane gliding by.
When he saw a flying elephant,
he shouted, "Oh, my!"

Turn the page.

[p. 16]
Next, Ellie met some jungle birds
and played dress-up with some feathers.
The birds taught Ellie how to chirp
so they could sing a song together.

Turn the page.

[p. 18]
The birds took Ellie around the world,
and showed her every place.
After she saw all that she wanted,
she soared all the way to space!

Aroo, aroo. Ellie is soaring. She is flying! Soar. Say soar. **PAUSE.** Soar means to fly. Tell me, what word means to fly? **PAUSE.** Soar! Nice work! Hmm. What are some things that soar? **PAUSE.** How about airplanes or helicopters? Those are things that fly! Now look behind the cloud to see something else that soars. **PAUSE.** It's a bird! It flies really high in the sky! Tell me, what does soar mean? **PAUSE.** To fly. Great job!

Turn the page.

[p. 20]
When Ellie got to space,
it was already night.
The sun was going down,
but the moon was shining bright.

Turn the page.

[p. 22]
When the moon had to go,
Ellie danced with the stars.
Then she started to fly home,
because space is very far.

Turn the page.

[p. 24]
Back home in the jungle,
only fireflies were awake,
so Ellie danced with them
above a shimmering lake.

Turn the page.

[p. 26]
Ellie had so much fun
pretending she could fly.
But she knew she would never
want to live in the sky.

Turn the page.

[p. 28]
Up in the sky,
Ellie would not have her friends.
So she was happy her adventures
were only pretend.

Turn the page.

[p. 30]
Ellie stopped imagining and thought,
"I am glad I cannot fly."
Then she snuggled down and fell asleep
with her friends by her side.

Aroo, aroo. That was a silly story. Ellie had a lot of fun pretending she could fly. Hmm. I have some questions for you. At the end of the story, Ellie Elephant was glad she cannot fly. Why was she glad? **PAUSE.** Because she would miss her friends! Her friends don't live in the sky. If Ellie could fly, she would not see them anymore. Ellie is very glad to be with her friends.

In this story, Ellie Elephant pretended she could fly. What do you like to pretend? **PAUSE.** I like to pretend I am a superhero! I can pretend I have special powers.

Turn the page.

Let's talk about the words we learned! Look at Marquez Monkey. Marquez is pretending he is running a race. He is imagining it! Say imagine. **PAUSE.** Tell me, what does imagine mean? **PAUSE.** To pretend. That's right!

One of our Jungle Friends can soar. Lift the flap to see. **PAUSE.** It's Tanisha Toucan! Tanisha flies in the sky. She soars! Say soar. **PAUSE.** Tell me, what does soar mean? **PAUSE.** To fly. Great job!

Turn the page.

Put your finger on the feather. Is a feather hard or soft? **PAUSE.** Soft!

Put your finger on the boards. Are the boards hard or soft? **PAUSE.** Hard. Good work!

I had a lot of fun with you in the Listening Center today! Thank you for coming! Raise your hand so your teacher knows you are finished. See you tomorrow!

Unit 2, Week 8

Leo Loses His Roar

Vocabulary: ill, comfort
Concept Words: empty, full

Aroo, aroo. Hello again. Welcome to the Listening Center. It's me, Wanda the Word Wolf. Do you have your book? **PAUSE.** Do you see a picture of Leo Lion on the cover? **PAUSE.** Yes! Now put your finger under the first word of the title. Follow the arrow under the words as we read the title of the book together. It says, *Leo Loses His Roar.*

Go ahead and open your book now.

Turn the page.

[p. 3]
Leo woke up one morning
and got out of bed.
He stretched and he yawned.
He had a big day ahead.

Turn the page.

[p. 5]
Leo was going to practice
his singing today.
Tomorrow he was singing
in the school play.

Turn the page.

[p. 6]
Suddenly, Leo noticed
something didn't feel right.
His nose felt stuffy.
His throat was itchy and tight.

Turn the page.

[p. 8]
Leo tried to roar
for his mother to come see.
But no sounds came out.
How could this be?

Turn the page.

[p. 10]
When Leo's mother came to find him,
he was still in bed.
Leo sneezed and sniffled.
"Are you feeling ill?" she said.

Aroo, aroo. Oh, no! Leo Lion is ill. He is sick. Ill. Say ill. **PAUSE.** Ill means sick. Tell me, what word means sick? **PAUSE.** Ill. That's right! Have you ever been ill and had to stay home sick from school? **PAUSE.** Maybe you had a tummy ache or a bad cough. That's no fun. Can you show me how you feel when you are ill? Put your hands on your tummy and pretend it hurts. Oh wow, you look sick! Tell me, what does ill mean? **PAUSE.** Sick. Good work!

Turn the page.

[p. 12]
Leo's mother said,
"Leo, it looks like you are sick.
Don't worry. I know exactly
what will do the trick."

Turn the page.

[p. 15]
Leo's mother asked his friends
to come over right away
to help him feel better
for tomorrow's school play.

Turn the page.

[p. 17]
Tanisha, Marquez,
and Ellie all agreed.
They would visit Leo
and help their friend in need.

Aroo, aroo. Leo Lion's friends are coming to see him. Why are they coming to see him? **PAUSE.** Because he is sick! Leo's friends want to help him feel better. I would like my friends to visit me if I was sick, too.

Turn the page.

[p. 18]
Tanisha brought berries
from the tallest jungle trees.
"Here, Leo, eat these berries.
They will help with your sneeze."

Turn the page.

[p. 20]
Marquez brought some soup
that was creamy and thick.
"Here, Leo, eat this soup.
It will soothe your throat quick."

Turn the page.

[p. 22]
Ellie brought a cold, wet cloth
to put on Leo's head.
She hoped that it would comfort him
as he rested in his bed.

Aroo, aroo. Leo's friends are comforting him. They are doing lots of things to make him feel better. Comfort. Say comfort. **PAUSE.** Comfort means to make you feel better. Tell me, what word means to make you feel better? **PAUSE.** Comfort. Great job! When I am sick, a nice warm blanket comforts me. It makes me feel better! I know something else that comforts me. Open the door to see. **PAUSE.** A hug! A hug makes me feel better. Tell me, what does comfort mean? **PAUSE.** To make you feel better. Awesome!

Turn the page.

[p. 25]
Leo's friends had one more thing
that they wanted to do.
They sang Leo's favorite song,
so he wouldn't feel blue.

Turn the page.

[p. 26]
The soup, cloth, and berries
helped Leo to rest.
But the song his friends sang
was the part he liked best.

Aroo, aroo. Look at Leo sleeping. Leo ate all his soup. The bowl is empty. Empty. Say empty. **PAUSE.** Now look in the basket. This bowl is full of soup. Full. Say full. **PAUSE.**

Turn the page.

[p. 29]
Soon Leo's friends
left him alone for the night.
After a long night of rest,
he woke up feeling just right.

Turn the page.

[p. 30]
On his way to school,
Leo practiced his song.
Then he let out a roar
that was mighty and strong.

Turn the page.

[p. 32]
On the stage at school,
Leo stood straight and tall.
When the play started,
Leo sang the loudest of all.

Aroo, aroo. Leo's friends came to visit him when he was sick. Hmm. I have some questions for you. At the end of the story, Leo Lion was happy! Why was Leo happy? **PAUSE.** Because he got to sing in the school play! Leo felt better, and he could sing his song.

In this story, Leo Lion's friends did nice things for him. Why should you do nice things for your friends? **PAUSE.** Because you care about your friends. Leo's friends helped him because they care about him. You should always help your friends.

Turn the page.

Let's talk about the words we learned! Look at the little boy blowing his nose. He looks sick. He is ill! Say ill. **PAUSE.** Tell me, what does ill mean? **PAUSE.** Sick. That's right!

Now look at the little boy with his teacher. The boy is sad, so his teacher is making him feel better. She is comforting him! Say comfort. **PAUSE.** Tell me, what does comfort mean? **PAUSE.** To make you feel better. Nice work!

Turn the page.

Open the blue door. I see a jar of jelly! Is it empty or full? **PAUSE.** Full! Now open the red door. Look at this jar. Is it empty or full? **PAUSE.** Empty. That's right!

I had a lot of fun with you in the Listening Center today! Thank you for coming! Raise your hand so your teacher knows you are finished. See you tomorrow!

Unit 2 Review, Week 9

Jungle Friends Go to the Park

Vocabulary Review: soar, ill, ruin, comfort, reckless, imagine

Aroo, aroo. Hello again! Welcome to the Listening Center. It's me, Wanda the Word Wolf. Remember, when you hear me say *Aroo, aroo,* it means it is time for you to answer some questions.

Do you have your book? **PAUSE.** Make sure it is closed, and do not open it until I tell you to. Look at the front cover of your book. Do you see a picture of the Jungle Friends on the cover? **PAUSE.** Yes! Now put your finger under the first word of the title. Follow the arrow under the words as we read the title of the book together. It says, *Jungle Friends Go to the Park.*

Go ahead and open your book now.

Turn the page.

[p. 2]
One morning, the Jungle Friends' teacher said they were going on a field trip.
"We are going to the park," said Ms. Hippo.
All the animals cheered!

Turn the page.

[p. 4]
The class lined up at the door.
Tanisha Toucan was the line leader.
Tanisha soared down the hall in front of the other animals.

Aroo, aroo. Look at Tanisha Toucan flying. She is soaring! Soar. Say soar. **PAUSE.** Soar means to fly. Tell me, what does soar mean? **PAUSE.** To fly. You got it!

Turn the page.

[p. 7]
There was a school bus waiting outside.
The animals stepped onto the bus one by one.

Turn the page.

[p. 8]
The bus drove down a bumpy road.
Leo Lion felt ill when the bus bounced up and down.
It made his tummy hurt.

Aroo, aroo. Oh, no! Leo Lion looks sick. He looks ill. Say ill. **PAUSE.** Ill means sick. Tell me, what does ill mean? **PAUSE.** Sick. That's right!

Turn the page.

[p. 10]
Soon, the animals arrived at the park.
Ms. Hippo said they were going to take a walk.
"There are lots of things to see!" she said.

Turn the page.

[p. 12]
First, the friends passed a pretty garden.
"Oh, look!" Marquez Monkey said.
A butterfly was flying from flower to flower.

Turn the page.

[p. 15]
Marquez chased the butterfly with his net, but he did not look where he was going.
He ran through the garden and smashed all the flowers.
Marquez ruined the flowers.

Aroo, aroo. Marquez messed up the flowers. He ruined them! Ruin. Say ruin. **PAUSE.** Ruin means to mess up. Tell me, what does ruin mean? **PAUSE.** To mess up. Good thinking!

Turn the page.

[p. 17]
"Uh-oh!" Ms. Hippo said. "What a mess!
No more playing in the garden."

Turn the page.

[p. 18]
Next, the friends walked deep into the jungle.
"Oh, look!" Marquez said.
There was something colorful resting on a leaf.
It was the butterfly!

Turn the page.

[p. 20]
Marquez chased the butterfly with his net, but he did not look where he was going.
Marquez tripped and skinned his knee.
Then he started to cry.

Turn the page.

[p. 23]
Tanisha Toucan comforted Marquez.
She hugged him and helped him get up.
Then Marquez felt better.

Aroo, aroo. Look at Tanisha Toucan. She is making Marquez feel better. She is comforting him. Comfort. Say comfort. **PAUSE.** Comfort means to make you feel better. Tell me, what does comfort mean? **PAUSE.** To make you feel better. Great job!

Turn the page.

[p. 24]
"Uh-oh!" Ms. Hippo said. "You got hurt.
No more running in the jungle."

Turn the page.

[p. 26]
Finally, the friends came
out of the jungle by a pond.
They climbed into a boat.
Ellie Elephant pushed the boat into the water and climbed in last.

Turn the page.

[p. 29]
Tanisha and Leo rowed the friends across the pond.
"Oh! Look!" Marquez said.
The butterfly was flying right by the boat!

Turn the page.

[p. 31]
Marquez stood on his tiptoes
and leaned over with his net.
Marquez really wanted to catch the butterfly,
but he was being reckless.
It was not safe to stand up in the boat.

Aroo, aroo. Uh-oh. Look at Marquez. He is not safe. He is being reckless. Say reckless. **PAUSE.** Reckless means not safe. Tell me, what does reckless mean? **PAUSE.** Not safe. Nice work!

Turn the page.

[p. 32]
SPLASH!
Marquez leaned too far and fell into the water.
The friends giggled.
Marquez looked funny when he was all wet.

Turn the page.

[p. 34]
Then Marquez made a fishy face.
He swam underwater and imagined he was a fish.
Marquez blew bubbles and waved at the real fish.
Pretending was fun!

Aroo, aroo. Marquez is pretending he's a fish. He's imagining it! Imagine. Say imagine. **PAUSE.** Imagine means to pretend. Tell me, what does imagine mean? **PAUSE.** To pretend. Great job!

Turn the page.

[p. 37]
"Uh-oh," Ms. Hippo said. "You are all wet!
No more swimming in the pond.
It's time to go back to school."
The friends followed their teacher back to the bus.

Turn the page.

[p. 38]
Just before the bus drove away,
the butterfly flew in the window.
It landed right on Marquez Monkey's head!

I had a lot of fun with you in the Listening Center today! Thank you for coming! Raise your hand so your teacher knows you are finished. See you tomorrow!

Unit 3, Week 10

Ellie Gets Stuck

Vocabulary: leap, pause
Concept Word: between

Aroo, aroo. Hello again. Welcome to the Listening Center. It's me, Wanda the Word Wolf. Do you have your book? **PAUSE.** Do you see a picture of Ellie Elephant on the cover? **PAUSE.** Yes! Now put your finger under the first word of the title. Follow the arrow under the words as we read the title of the book together. It says, *Ellie Gets Stuck.*

Go ahead and open your book now.

Turn the page.

[p. 3]
Ellie met her friends
in the jungle one day.
There were so many games
they wanted to play!

Turn the page.

[p. 5]
The friends all agreed
that playing tag would be fun.
Ellie said, "Leo, you're it!
Everybody run!"

Turn the page.

[p. 6]
Marquez was fast,
but Leo followed his trail.
Leo leapt far and tagged
Marquez on the tail.

Aroo, aroo. Leo leapt to get Marquez. He jumped! Leap. Say leap. **PAUSE.** Leap means to jump. Tell me, what word means to jump? **PAUSE.** Leap. That's right! What are some things you know that leap? **PAUSE.** Hmm. I have some ideas. Rabbits leap, and so do frogs. They both jump! Pretend that your hand is a frog. Make the frog leap. Make it jump across your book. Tell me, what does leap mean? **PAUSE.** To jump. Great job!

Turn the page.

[p. 9]
Now Marquez was it.
It was his turn to chase.
He chased his friend Ellie
all over the place.

Turn the page.

[p. 11]
"Tag! You're it!" said Marquez.
"Catch us if you can!"
Then Ellie began to chase
Tanisha Toucan.

Aroo, aroo. The Jungle Friends are playing tag. What game do you like to play? **PAUSE.** I like to play Hide and Seek or have a race with my friends!

Turn the page.

[p. 13]
Ellie noticed that Tanisha
was flying too fast.
But she knew if she tried,
she would catch her at last.

Turn the page.

[p. 14]
Between two tall trees,
Tanisha swiftly flew.
But Ellie was afraid
that she might not fit through!

Turn the page.

[p. 17]
Ellie tried to jump between the trees,
but she didn't have much luck.
She was too big to fit through,
and now she was stuck.

Turn the page.

[p. 19]
Soon Marquez paused to rest
for a minute or two.
He leaned up against something
Big, round, and blue.

Aroo, aroo. Marquez paused and leaned on Ellie. He stopped. Pause. Say pause. **PAUSE.** Pause means to stop. Tell me, what word means to stop? **PAUSE.** Pause. Good work. If you are playing on the playground and you get tired, you might pause. You might stop. Let's play a game. You will tap your finger on your book until I say Pause. When I say pause, you stop. Okay? Let's start. Tap your finger. **PAUSE.** Pause! Did you stop? Tap your finger again. **PAUSE.** Now pause! I hope you stopped. Great job! Tell me, what does pause mean? **PAUSE.** To stop.

Turn the page.

[p. 20]
When he noticed it was Ellie,
stuck between the trees,
Marquez cried, "Tanisha! Leo!
Come help us, please!"

Turn the page.

[p. 23]
"Since Ellie is big,
and we are very small,
we must work together.
Our friend needs us all!"

Aroo, aroo. Oh, no! Ellie is still stuck between the trees. Between. Say between. **PAUSE.** I have an idea. Put your hands between your knees. Pretend they are stuck like Ellie. Now let them go. Whew!

Turn the page.

[p. 24]
So Leo pulled on Ellie's trunk.
He held on very tight.
Marquez pushed Ellie from behind.
He pushed with all his might.

Turn the page.

[p. 26]
Marquez said, "One more push
is all that we need.
Then our good friend Ellie
will soon be freed."

Turn the page.

[p. 29]
"Okay!" Tanisha said.
"I'll give it a try!"
She flew up in the air
so fast and so high.

Turn the page.

[p. 30]
She hit Ellie from behind
with a loud jungle crash.
Then Ellie Elephant
was free in a flash!

Turn the page.

[p. 32]
Ellie laughed as the
Jungle Friends lay in a pile.
She said, "I don't think I will jump
through any trees for a while."

Aroo, aroo. Wow. What a good story! Ellie got stuck, but all her friends helped her. Hmm. I have some questions for you. The friends all tried to help Ellie Elephant. Why did they help Ellie? **PAUSE.** Because she couldn't get out by herself. She was stuck! The friends were worried, so they worked together to get Ellie out.

Do you think Ellie Elephant will try to jump between the trees again? **PAUSE.** No, I don't think she will. Ellie learned that she might get stuck if she jumps between the trees. She won't want to get stuck again.

Turn the page.

Let's talk about the words we learned! Look at the boys. They are jumping off a bench. They are leaping. Say leap. **PAUSE.** Tell me, what does leap mean? **PAUSE.** To jump. Great work!

Look at the little boy with the stop sign. He is telling you to stop. He is telling you to pause. Say Pause. **PAUSE.** Tell me, what does pause mean? **PAUSE.** To stop. Awesome!

Turn the page.

Look at the picture of the boy and the dogs. Is the boy between the dogs or on top of the dogs? **PAUSE.** Between the dogs. Good work!

I had a lot of fun with you in the Listening Center today! Thank you for coming! Raise your hand so your teacher knows you are finished. See you tomorrow!

Unit 3, Week 11

A New Jungle Friend

Vocabulary: speedy, wise
Concept Word: around

Aroo, aroo. Hello again. Welcome to the Listening Center. It's me, Wanda the Word Wolf. Do you have your book? **PAUSE.** Do you see a picture of a green snake on the cover? **PAUSE.** Yes! Now put your finger under the first word of the title. Follow the arrow under the words as we read the title of the book together. It says, *A New Jungle Friend.*

Go ahead and open your book now.

Turn the page.

[p. 3]
One morning, the friends met
in the jungle to play.
Each animal came
in its own special way.

Turn the page.

[p. 5]
Marquez Monkey swung
from tree to tree.
Tanisha Toucan flew
as fast as could be.

Turn the page.

[p. 6]
Ellie marched noisily
through the mud.
With each step, her feet
made a thump and a thud.

Turn the page.

[p. 8]
Leo ran with great speed
and let out a loud roar.
Then he looked down and saw something
he'd never seen before.

Turn the page.

[p. 11]
"Wow, Ellie!
Your footprints are huge!" Leo said.
"Look at this one.
It's even bigger than my head!"

Turn the page.

[p. 12]
Leo said, "I wish my feet
were big like yours."
"But why?" Ellie asked.
"You can run so fast and roar!"

Turn the page.

[p. 14]
"Yeah," Marquez said,
"Leo is faster than everyone.
I wish I was speedy.
I could have so much fun!"

Aroo, aroo. Marquez wishes he was speedy. He wishes he was fast. Speedy. Say speedy. **PAUSE.** Speedy means fast. Tell me, what word means fast? **PAUSE.** Speedy. Great job! Can you tell me some things that are speedy? **PAUSE.** Hmm. A car can be speedy. When you run really fast, you are speedy. Look! Leo and Marquez are going to have a race. Help Leo be speedy. Put your finger on Leo. Ready, set, go! Wow! They sure are speedy. Tell me, what does speedy mean? **PAUSE.** Fast. That's right!

Turn the page.

[p. 16]
Leo said, "But Marquez,
you can swing through the trees.
You can swing high or low,
or anywhere you please."

Turn the page.

[p. 18]
"Yeah," Tanisha said,
"I wish I could swing around."
"Why?" said Marquez.
"You can fly above the ground."

Aroo, aroo. Tanisha Toucan wishes she was different. Why does she wish she was different? **PAUSE.** Because her friends can do some special things that she can't do. She wishes she could swing around like Marquez.

Turn the page.

[p. 20]
Ellie said, "I wish I could fly
high up in the air.
But I have big feet instead of wings.
It just doesn't seem fair."

Turn the page.

[p. 23]
A long green snake was listening
in a tree overhead.
The snake had heard everything
that the friends had said.

Aroo, aroo. Look at the snake! He is wrapped around the tree. Around. Say around. **PAUSE.** Now, can you draw a circle around Leo? Use your finger to go all the way around him. **PAUSE.** Great job!

Turn the page.

[p. 24]
The snake said, "I don't have big feet.
I can't fly, swing, or run.
But I don't wish to be someone else,
because being me is fun."

Turn the page.

[p. 26]
"Everyone is special.
No one else is just like me.
I have a long, strong body
that can slither up a tree."

Turn the page.

[p. 28]
The snake smiled at the friends,
and then he closed his eyes.
He knew so much about being special.
He was very wise.

Aroo, aroo. The snake is wise. He is smart. Wise. Say wise. **PAUSE.** Wise means smart. Tell me, what word means smart? **PAUSE.** Wise. Nice thinking! Who do you know who is wise? **PAUSE.** I bet your grandma or grandpa is wise. I bet they are smart and know a lot of things. Lift the flap to see someone else who is wise. **PAUSE.** It's a teacher! Teachers are smart. They help you learn. Tell me, what does wise mean? **PAUSE.** Smart. That's right!

Turn the page.

[p. 30]
The friends listened carefully
to what the snake had to say.
Then they agreed that we're each special
in our own way.

Aroo, aroo. The friends had a fun day in the jungle. They met a new friend! Hmm. I have some questions for you. What did the Jungle Friends learn from the snake? **PAUSE.** They learned that everyone is different and special! Leo can run really fast, and Tanisha can fly. The snake taught them to be happy about the special things they can do.

The Jungle Friends can each do something special. What is something special that you can do? **PAUSE.** I can play the drums. I am a good swimmer, too! Those are things I can do that make me special.

Turn the page.

Let's talk about the words we learned!

Look at the picture of the airplanes. They are really fast. They are speedy. Say speedy. **PAUSE.** Tell me, what does speedy mean? **PAUSE.** Fast. That's right!

Look at the picture of the doctor. The doctor knows a lot about keeping you healthy. He is smart. He is wise. Say wise. **PAUSE.** Tell me, what does wise mean? **PAUSE.** Smart. Nice thinking!

Turn the page.

Look at Marquez Monkey and the flower. Do you see the bees? **PAUSE.** Are the bees around the flower or on the flower? **PAUSE.** Around the flower. That's right!

I had a lot of fun with you in the Listening Center today! Thank you for coming! Raise your hand so your teacher knows you are finished. See you tomorrow!

Unit 3, Week 12

Marquez's Backwards Day

Vocabulary: ridiculous, tumble
Concept Words: day, night

Aroo, aroo. Hello again. Welcome to the Listening Center. It's me, Wanda the Word Wolf. Do you have your book? **PAUSE.** Do you see a picture of Marquez Monkey on the cover? **PAUSE.** Yes! Now put your finger under the first word of the title. Follow the arrow under the words as we read the title of the book together. It says, *Marquez's Backwards Day.*

Go ahead and open your book now.

Turn the page.

[p. 2]
Marquez jumped out of bed one morning
and got ready to play!
This monkey was feeling
extra silly today.

Turn the page.

[p. 4]
"I want to do things backwards today,"
Marquez said.
So he wore hats on his feet
and a boot on his head!

Turn the page.

[p. 7]
How ridiculous!
Why was he acting this way?
Marquez told his mother
it was backwards day!

Aroo, aroo. Look at Marquez! He is ridiculous! He's silly. Ridiculous. Say ridiculous. **PAUSE.** Ridiculous means silly. Tell me, what word means silly? **PAUSE.** Ridiculous. That's right! Marquez was wearing hats on his feet and a boot on his head. That's ridiculous! That's silly! What if...you wore your clothes in the bathtub?

PAUSE. That's ridiculous! Now lift the flap to see something else that is ridiculous. **PAUSE.** Look! A dog dressed up like a princess! That's silly. Say, "That's ridiculous!" **PAUSE.** Tell me, what does ridiculous mean? **PAUSE.** Silly. Nice work!

Turn the page.

[p. 8]
When Marquez met his friends,
he waved and said, "Goodbye!
On backwards day, friends,
that means you're saying, 'Hi!'"

Turn the page.

[p. 10]
Then Marquez began to swing
backwards through the trees.
"Marquez, be careful!" Leo cried.
"Turn around, please!"

Aroo, aroo. Leo Lion told Marquez Monkey to turn around. Why did he tell Marquez that? **PAUSE.** Because he doesn't want Marquez to get hurt! Marquez is swinging backwards, and Leo thinks he might hurt himself.

Turn the page.

[p. 13]
CRASH!
Marquez ran into a tree!
Then he said in a silly way,
"Haven't you heard, Leo?
Today is backwards day!"

Turn the page.

[p. 15]
When the friends went to the park,
they thought the slide looked fun.
Ellie, Leo, and Tanisha
slid down one by one.

Turn the page.

[p. 17]
But Marquez was feeling silly,
so he ran up the slide.
Then he climbed down the ladder
that was on the other side.

Turn the page.

[p. 19]
When Tanisha asked why
he was acting this way,
Marquez said, "Haven't you heard?
Today is backwards day!"

Turn the page.

[p. 20]
The friends thought running up a slide
was a silly thing to do.
But since it looked like fun,
they decided to try it, too.

Turn the page.

[p. 22]
Running up a slide
is not as easy as going down.
So Marquez bumped his head
as the friends tumbled to the ground.

Aroo, aroo. Uh-oh. The Jungle Friends tumbled off the slide. They fell! Tumble. Say tumble. **PAUSE.** Tumble means to fall. Tell me, what word means to fall? **PAUSE.** Tumble. That's right! Have you ever tumbled off the bed or tumbled down the stairs? **PAUSE.** Maybe you have tumbled on the playground at school. Oops! You fell. Lift the flap and look at the pictures of Ellie. **PAUSE.** Point to the picture that shows Ellie tumbling. Did you point to Ellie falling out of her chair? **PAUSE.** Good job! Tell me, what does tumble mean? **PAUSE.** To fall. Great thinking!

Turn the page.

[p. 24]
When it was time to go home,
Marquez said, "Hello!
On backwards day, friends,
that means it's time to go."

Turn the page.

[p. 27]
Marquez made it home,
walking backwards the whole way.
Then he told his mother
all about his backwards day.

Aroo, aroo. Marquez played all day! Day. Say day. **PAUSE.** Lift the window! **PAUSE.** I see the sun! The sun shines during the day! In the story, Marquez is at home. Almost time to go to bed, it is night! Night. Say night. **PAUSE.**

Turn the page.

[p. 29]
"Doing things backwards is difficult,"
Mother said.
"You crashed into a tree,
fell off the slide, and bumped your head!"

Turn the page.

[p. 30]
"Don't worry," Marquez said.
"See? I'm okay.
Do you know what tomorrow is?
It's upside-down day!"

Aroo, aroo. What a funny story! Marquez did everything backwards. Hmm. I have some questions for you. The Jungle Friends thought Marquez was silly. Why did they think he was silly? **PAUSE.** Because he was doing everything backwards! He was walking backwards and swinging backwards, and he said, "Goodbye" instead of "Hi."

Do you think Marquez Monkey will have another backwards day? **PAUSE.** Yes, I think he will! Marquez had so much fun doing everything backwards. He will probably want to do it again.

Turn the page. Let's talk about the words we learned!

Look at the picture of the boy in the funny glasses. He is silly. He is ridiculous! Say ridiculous. **PAUSE.** Tell me, what does ridiculous mean? **PAUSE.** Silly. Great job!

Look at the Jungle Friends. They fell onto the sand. They tumbled. Say tumble. **PAUSE.** Tell me, what does tumble mean? **PAUSE.** To fall. That's right!

Turn the page.

Put your finger on the picture where the sun is shining. Is it day or night? **PAUSE.** Day. Good work!

Now put your finger on the picture where you can see the moon. Is it day or night? **PAUSE.** Night. That's right!

I had a lot of fun with you in the Listening Center today! Thank you for coming! Raise your hand so your teacher knows you are finished. See you tomorrow!

Unit 3 Review, Week 13

Jungle Friends Swing Through the Vines

Vocabulary Review: wise, pause, leap, speedy, ridiculous, tumble

Aroo, aroo. Hello again! Welcome to the Listening Center. It's me, Wanda the Word Wolf. Remember, when you hear me say *Aroo, aroo,* it means it is time for you to answer some questions.

Do you have your book? **PAUSE.** Make sure it is closed, and do not open it until I tell you to. Look at the front cover of your book. Do you see a picture of the Jungle Friends on the cover? **PAUSE.** Yes! Now put your finger under the first word of the title. Follow the arrow under the words as we read the title of the book together. It says, *Jungle Friends Swing Through the Vines.*

Go ahead and open your book now.

Turn the page.

[p. 3]
It was a beautiful day in the jungle.
The Jungle Friends were trying to think
of something fun to do.

Turn the page.

[p. 5]
Ellie Elephant had an idea.
"Let's have a race," she said.
"Let's swing on vines and race through the trees!"
"Great idea!" cheered the friends.

Turn the page.

[p. 7]
"I can help. I will be your coach!"
said Tanisha Toucan.
Tanisha was wise.
She knew a lot about flying through the jungle.
Tanisha would be a great coach
because she was so smart.

Aroo, aroo. Tanisha Toucan is smart. She is wise. Say wise. **PAUSE.** Wise means smart. Tell me, what does wise mean? **PAUSE.** Smart. You got it!

Turn the page.

[p. 8]
First, the friends had to find
a good place to start the race.
Tanisha pointed to a big rock with lots of vines near it.
"Follow me!" she said as she flew to the top.

Turn the page.

[p. 11]
Leo, Marquez, and Ellie stood by the rock.
But they were so excited to race,
they wouldn't listen to their coach.
They kept playing on the vines
and being very loud!

Turn the page.

[p. 12]
So Coach Tanisha blew her whistle loudly.
[Whistle]
The friends finally stopped playing around.
They paused to listen to Tanisha.

Aroo, aroo. Look! The friends stopped playing. They paused. Pause. Say pause. **PAUSE.** Pause means to stop. Tell me, what does pause mean? **PAUSE.** To stop. Nice thinking!

Turn the page.

[p. 15]
Coach Tanisha explained the rules of the game.
"Follow the red flags and swing from vine to vine.
Whoever reaches the last flag first is the winner!"

Turn the page.

[p. 16]
"But remember," Tanisha said,
"hold on tight
and always watch where you are going.
On your mark ... get set ... GO!"

Turn the page.

[p. 19]
Marquez Monkey was the first one to leap on the vine.
He jumped far out, swung through the air,
and caught another vine.

Aroo, aroo. Point to Marquez Monkey jumping on the vine. He is leaping! Leap. Say leap. **PAUSE.** Leap means to jump. Tell me, what does leap mean? **PAUSE.** To jump. That's right!

Turn the page.

[p. 20]
Marquez swung quickly from vine to vine.
"I am so good at swinging," he thought.
"I know I'm going to win the race."
Then Marquez looked behind him
and got a big surprise.

Turn the page.

[p. 22]
Oh, no! Leo Lion was fast.
Leo was so speedy,
he had almost caught Marquez!
And Ellie Elephant was not far behind.

Aroo, aroo. Look at Leo Lion swinging. He is so fast. He is speedy. Say speedy. **PAUSE.** Speedy means fast. Tell me, what does speedy mean? **PAUSE.** Fast. Great job!

Turn the page.

[p. 25]
Then Marquez Monkey got an idea.
If Leo and Ellie let go of their vines,
He would win the race.

Turn the page.

[p. 26]
So Marquez turned toward his friends
and made a ridiculous face.
Marquez Monkey looked so silly
that Leo and Ellie started to laugh and laugh.

Aroo, aroo. Do you see Marquez Monkey's face? It is silly. It is ridiculous! Say ridiculous. **PAUSE.** Ridiculous means silly. Tell me, what does ridiculous mean? **PAUSE.** Silly. Good work!

Turn the page.

[p. 28]
When Marquez saw his friends laughing,
he started to laugh, too!
They all laughed so hard that they let go of their vines.
All the Jungle Friends tumbled to the ground!

Aroo, aroo. Uh-oh! The friends fell off their vines. They tumbled. Tumble. Say tumble. **PAUSE.** Tumble means to fall. Tell me, what does tumble mean? **PAUSE.** To fall. Awesome job!

Turn the page.

[p. 31]
The friends fell right in front of the last red flag.
"No one made it to the finish!"
Coach Tanisha said.
"You let go of your vines too soon."

Turn the page.

[p. 32]
The Jungle Friends laughed some more.
They all agreed they had so much fun,
it didn't matter that no one won the race.

I had a lot of fun with you in the Listening Center today! Thank you for coming! Raise your hand so your teacher knows you are finished. See you tomorrow!

Unit 4, Week 14

Meet the Forest Friends

Aroo, aroo. Hello. Welcome to the Listening Center. Do you have your book? **PAUSE.** Make sure it is closed, and do not open it until I tell you to. Look at the front cover of your book. Do you see a picture of animals on the cover? **PAUSE.** Yes! Do you see some words there at the top? **PAUSE.** This is the name of the book. The name of a book is called the title. Now, put your finger under the first word of the title. Follow the arrow under the words as we read the title of the book together. It says, *Meet the Forest Friends.*

Go ahead and open your book now.

Hello again! My name is Wanda the Word Wolf. Do you see me? I have pointy ears and a fluffy tail. What is your name? **PAUSE.** Great! It's nice to meet you.

Every time you come to the Listening Center, you will get a book to read with me. And when you hear me say *Aroo, aroo,* it means it is time for you to listen and answer some questions. Let's practice.

Aroo, aroo. Did you hear me say *Aroo, aroo*? **PAUSE.** Let's answer a question. Are you ready? **PAUSE.** Okay! Here's one: How old are you? **PAUSE.** Great job! Now, point to my nose. What color is my nose? **PAUSE.** Black. That's right!

In this book, we are going to meet some more new friends. When you hear this sound it means you can go ahead and turn the page. Let's turn the page now.

Turn the page.

Do you see the picture of the forest? **PAUSE.** A forest is a shady place with lots of trees, plants, and animals. Today you will meet four animals called the Forest Friends! First is Pablo Porcupine. He has a soccer ball. Point to Pablo Porcupine. **PAUSE.** Next is Fae Fox. She is holding a balloon. Point to Fae Fox. **PAUSE.** Bobby Bear is holding a leaf. Do you see him? Point to Bobby Bear. **PAUSE.** Last is Suki Squirrel. She is hanging from a tree branch. Point to Suki Squirrel. **PAUSE.**

Great listening! Let's start our story now.

Turn the page.

[p. 5]
The Forest Friends are waking up.
A porcupine, a fox, a squirrel, and a bear.
It is their first day of school,
and they are excited to get there!

Turn the page.

[p. 7]
Fae Fox is leaving her den.
She does not want to be late.
"Hooray!" she says. "It's time for school.
I cannot wait!"

Aroo, aroo. Did you hear me say *Aroo, aroo*? **PAUSE.** Let's answer a question. Are you ready? **PAUSE.** Fae Fox is leaving for school. But she forgot something. Look behind the rock to find it. **PAUSE.** What did Fae forget? **PAUSE.** Her backpack! Thanks for helping.

Turn the page.

[p. 8]
Bobby Bear is leaving his house, too.
He does not want to be late.
"Yeah!" he says. "It's time for school.
I cannot wait!"

Aroo, aroo. Lift the flap to see what Bobby wants to play at the school playground. **PAUSE.** Basketball! Bobby wants to play basketball. What do you like to play at the playground? **PAUSE.** I like to play on the jungle gym.

Turn the page.

[p. 11]
Suki Squirrel is leaving her tree.
She does not want to be late.
"Woohoo!" she says. "It is time for school.
I cannot wait!"

Aroo, aroo. Look! Suki Squirrel is waving bye to her mom. Can you wave to Suki's mom, too? Wave and say bye bye! **PAUSE.** That's nice!

Turn the page.

[p. 13]
Pablo Porcupine is leaving his burrow.
He does not want to be late.
"Yippee!" he says. "It's time for school.
I cannot wait!"

Aroo, aroo. I wonder what's in Pablo Porcupine's backpack. Lift the flap to see what he is taking to school. **PAUSE.** I see a lunchbox. Say lunchbox. **PAUSE.** I see a book. Say book. **PAUSE.** Good work!

Turn the page.

[p. 14]
Pablo, Suki, Bobby, and Fae
found their way.
They are so excited for
their first school day!

Aroo, aroo. The Forest Friends made it to their classroom. They look happy. Why are the Forest Friends happy? **PAUSE.** Because it's their first day of school!

You did a great job answering questions today! Now, can you find me, Wanda the Word Wolf, on this page? **PAUSE.** Remember, every time you come to the Listening Center, you will get a book to read with me. And when you hear me say *Aroo, aroo,* it means it is time for you to listen and answer some questions.

I had so much fun with you at the Listening Center today! Thank you for coming! Raise your hand so your teacher knows you are finished. See you tomorrow!

Unit 4, Week 15

Pablo's Prickly Problem

Vocabulary: terrified, protect
Concept Words: largest, smallest

Aroo, aroo. Hello again. Welcome to the Listening Center. It's me, Wanda the Word Wolf. Remember, when you hear me say *Aroo, aroo,* it means it is time for you to answer some questions.

Do you have your book? **PAUSE.** Make sure it is closed, and do not open it until I tell you to. Look at the front cover of your book. Do you see a picture of Pablo Porcupine on the cover? **PAUSE.** Yes! Now put your finger under the first word of the title. Follow the arrow under the words as we read the title of the book together. It says, *Pablo's Prickly Problem.*

Go ahead and open your book now.

Pablo is a porcupine. Here is a picture of a real porcupine. A porcupine is covered with quills. Quills are pointy and sharp. Do you see the quills on your page? **PAUSE.** They are quills from a real porcupine. Do they look pointy and sharp? **PAUSE.** Yes, they do!

Turn the page.

[p. 3]
One day Pablo Porcupine
awoke ready to play.
"Remember," Mother said,
"school starts today."

Turn the page.

[p. 4]
Pablo got so excited.
He could hardly wait!
It was almost time to leave,
and he did not want to be late.

Turn the page.

[p. 7]
Pablo brushed his teeth
and washed his face.
He combed his quills
so they would stay in place.

Turn the page.

[p. 9]
When Pablo got to school,
he opened the door.
He saw lots of different animals
he had never seen before.

Turn the page.

[p. 11]
Some animals were large,
and others were small.
But no one looked like Pablo,
not even at all.

Aroo, aroo. Look at the animals in the classroom. The animals are all different sizes. Put your finger on Bobby Bear! He is the largest. Say largest. **PAUSE.** Now put your finger on Suki Squirrel. She is the smallest. Say smallest. **PAUSE.** Good work!

Turn the page.

[p. 13]
"Oh, no! I'm the only one with quills,"
Pablo thought.
"All the other animals have soft fur,
but I do not."

Aroo, aroo. Pablo Porcupine is sad. Why is Pablo sad? **PAUSE.** Because he doesn't look like the other animals. He's the only one with quills. The other animals have fur.

Turn the page.

[p. 14]
Then Pablo found his desk
and tucked away his books.
The animals in his class
were giving him strange looks.

Turn the page.

[p. 17]
The other animals were terrified
when Pablo sat down in his chair.
They noticed Pablo's quills,
and they were very scared.

Aroo, aroo. Look at Bobby Bear hiding behind the desk. He is terrified! He is really scared. Terrified. Say terrified. **PAUSE.** Terrified means really scared. Tell me, what word means really scared? **PAUSE.** Terrified. That's right! If your friend jumped out and said, "Boo!" you might be terrified! You might be really scared if your friend surprised you. Open the door. **PAUSE.** See the little boy? He looks terrified! He is really scared. Now, you make a terrified face. **PAUSE.** Wow! You look really scared! Say, "I'm terrified!" **PAUSE.** Tell me, what does terrified mean? **PAUSE.** Really scared. Great work!

Turn the page.

[p. 19]
The animals shot hoops at playtime,
but Pablo stood alone.
Then Bobby Bear lost control
of the ball that he had thrown.

Turn the page.

[p. 20]
The ball landed on Pablo's quills,
and it went POP!
Nobody budged.
The playing came to a stop.

Turn the page.

[p. 25]
The animals were scared.
They looked at Pablo with fright.
"Don't worry," Pablo said.
"Everything will be all right!"

Turn the page.

[p. 24]
"I will not hurt you.
I would not hurt a flea!
My quills are only here
to help protect me."

Aroo, aroo. Pablo said that his quills protect him. They keep him safe. Protect. Say protect. **PAUSE.** Protect means to keep someone safe. What word means to keep someone safe? **PAUSE.** Protect! That's right! You might wear a helmet to protect you when you ride your bike! Your helmet keeps you safe. When you are in the car, you put your seatbelt on to protect you. Pretend you are putting on your seatbelt. **PAUSE.** Click! Great job! Tell me, what does protect mean? **PAUSE.** To keep someone safe.

Turn the page.

[p. 27]
Then the animals came closer,
one by one.
Suki Squirrel said,
"Pablo, come join in our fun!"

Turn the page.

[p. 28]
Pablo and Suki played
with Bobby Bear and a fox named Fae.
And they all became friends,
even though no one looked the same way.

Aroo, aroo. What a great story. Pablo and the other animals became friends! Hmm. I have some questions for you. At the beginning of the story, the other animals in Pablo Porcupine's class were afraid of him. Why were they afraid of Pablo? **PAUSE.** Because Pablo was different. Pablo had quills! I bet they were afraid that his sharp, pointy quills would hurt them.

Remember when Suki Squirrel asked Pablo Porcupine to play? Why did Suki ask Pablo to play? **PAUSE.** Because she wanted Pablo to be her friend! Suki wasn't afraid of Pablo anymore. She wanted to be nice to him.

Turn the page.

Let's talk about the words we learned. Look at the picture of Fae Fox and Suki Squirrel. They are really scared! They are terrified! Say terrified. **PAUSE.** Tell me, what does terrified mean? **PAUSE.** Really scared! That's right!

Look at the picture of the little girl. Her mom is holding her hand to keep her safe. She is protecting her while they cross the street. Say protect. **PAUSE.** Tell me, what does protect mean? **PAUSE.** To keep someone safe. Great job!

Turn the page.

Put your finger on the cat. Is it the largest or the smallest? **PAUSE.** It is the largest! Great job. Now put your finger on the bee. Is it the largest or the smallest? **PAUSE.** It is the smallest. Awesome!

I had a lot of fun with you in the Listening Center today! Thank you for coming! Raise your hand so your teacher knows you are finished. See you tomorrow!*

Unit 4, Week 16

Suki's Sleepover Surprise

Vocabulary: agree, disappointed
Concept Words: first, last

Aroo, aroo. Hello again. Welcome to the Listening Center. It's me, Wanda the Word Wolf. Remember, when you hear me say *Aroo, aroo,* it means it is time for you to answer some questions.

Do you have your book? **PAUSE.** Make sure it is closed and do not open it until I tell you to. Look at the front cover of your book. Do you see a picture of Suki Squirrel on the cover? **PAUSE.** Yes! Now put your finger under the first word of the title. Follow the arrow under the words as we read the title of the book together. It says, *Suki's Sleepover Surprise.*

Go ahead and open your book now.

Turn the page.

[p. 3]
Suki Squirrel woke up one morning
and got out of bed.
"It would be fun
to have a sleepover," she said.

Turn the page.

[p. 4]
Suki asked her mom,
"Can I have a sleepover in our tree?"
Suki smiled and said, "Pleeease,"
and got her mom to agree.

Aroo, aroo. Suki's mom agreed! Her mom said yes to the party. Agree. Say agree. **PAUSE.** Agree means to say yes. Tell me, what word means to say yes? **PAUSE.** Agree! When you ask if you can play outside, and you mom says yes, she agrees! I like playing outside. Do you? **PAUSE.** If you said yes, *you* agree! Nod your head up and down, up and down. Say "Yes, I agree!" **PAUSE.** Tell me, what does "agree" mean? **PAUSE.** To say yes. Way to go!

Turn the page.

[p. 6]
Suki was so excited!
She called each friend, one by one.
She hoped they all could come.
It would be so much fun!

Aroo, aroo. Suki Squirrel is excited. Why is Suki excited? **PAUSE.** Because she thinks her friends will come over. Suki thinks it will be lots of fun to see her friends.

Turn the page.

[p. 9]
First, Suki called Fae Fox.
But Fae said she could not go.
Suki was SO sad.
Why did Fae say no?

Turn the page.

[p. 11]
Next, Suki called Bobby Bear.
But Bobby said he could not go.
Suki was SO sad.
Why did Bobby say no?

Turn the page.

[p. 13]
Last, Suki called Pablo Porcupine.
But Pablo said he could not go.
Suki was SO sad.
Why did Pablo say no?

Aroo, aroo. Suki called all her friends to come to the sleepover, and she is sad because they said no. Point to Fae Fox. Suki called Fae first. Say, first. **PAUSE.** Now, point to Pablo Porcupine. Suki called Pablo last. Say last. **PAUSE.** Great! Let's see what happens next.

Turn the page.

[p. 15]
Suki was so disappointed.
No one could come and stay.
She just wanted this
to be a special day.

Aroo, aroo. Suki was so disappointed. She was sad that her friends couldn't come to her sleepover. Disappointed. Say disappointed. **PAUSE.** Disappointed means sad. Tell me, what word means sad? **PAUSE.** Disappointed. Great job! If you wanted to go the playground, but it started to rain, you would be disappointed. You would be sad that you didn't get to play. Now make a disappointed face. Say, "I'm disappointed." **PAUSE.** Tell me, what does disappointed mean? **PAUSE.** Sad. That's right!

Turn the page.

[p. 17]
Then Suki's mother asked,
"Why are you crying, dear?"
"I want to have a sleepover," said Suki,
"but no one can come here."

Turn the page.

[p. 18]
"Try not to be too sad,"
Suki's mother said.
"Why don't we go
to the movies instead?"

Turn the page.

[p. 20]
So Suki and her mom
saw a movie later that day.
But Suki was still sad her friends
could not come over and stay.

Turn the page.

[p. 22]
When Suki returned home,
it was as dark as could be.
She flipped on the lights,
and what did she see?

Turn the page.

[p. 24]
SURPRISE!
Pablo, Fae, and Bobby
all were there!
Suki Squirrel was so happy
she jumped up into the air!

Turn the page.

[p. 26]
The friends ate popcorn
and watched cartoons all night!
Then Fae read a bedtime story,
while Suki held the light.

Turn the page.

[p. 28]
Suki Squirrel said,
as she closed her eyes,
"This was the greatest sleepover—
a perfect surprise!"

Aroo, aroo. Suki and her friends had fun at the sleepover! Hmm. I have some questions for you. Suki Squirrel's mom took her to the movies. Why did she take Suki to the movies? **PAUSE.** Because she didn't want Suki to be too sad! Suki was sad that her friends could not come over. Suki's mom took her to the movies so Suki would feel better.

The Forest Friends watched cartoons and read a story at Suki's sleepover. What do you like to do with your friends? **PAUSE.** I like to play games and draw pictures with my friends.

Turn the page.

Let's talk about the words we learned. Look! Now Suki is calling you on the phone! *"Hello? Can you come to my party?"* Say, "Yes! I agree." **PAUSE.** Agree. Say agree. **PAUSE.** Tell me, what does agree mean? **PAUSE.** To say yes. Nice work!

Now, look at the picture of the little girl. She is sad because she was late to school and missed playtime. She doesn't get to play with her favorite toys. She is disappointed! Say disappointed. **PAUSE.** Tell me, what does disappointed mean? **PAUSE.** Sad. Great thinking!

Turn the page.

Look at the Forest Friends walking in a line to Suki's tree. Point to Bobby Bear. Is Bobby first or last? **PAUSE.** First. Bobby Bear is first. Now point to Pablo Porcupine. Is Pablo first or last? **PAUSE.** Last. Great thinking!

I had so much fun with you at the Listening Center today! Thank you for coming. Raise your hand so your teacher knows you are finished. See you tomorrow!

Unit 4, Week 17

Bobby's EmBEARassing Visit

Vocabulary: kind, accident
Concept Words: tall, short

Aroo, aroo. Hello again. Welcome to the Listening Center. It's me, Wanda the Word Wolf. Remember, when you hear me say *Aroo, aroo,* it means it is time for you to answer some questions.

Do you have your book? **PAUSE.** Make sure it is closed, and do not open it until I tell you to. Look at the front cover of your book. Do you see a picture of Bobby Bear on the cover? **PAUSE.** Yes! Now put your finger under the first word of the title. Follow the arrow under the words as we read the title of the book together. It says, *Bobby's EmBEARassing Visit.*

Go ahead and open your book now.

Have you ever been to the doctor? **PAUSE.** A doctor looks in your mouth and ears and measures how tall you are. In this story, Bobby Bear is going to the doctor. Let's see what happens.

Turn the page.

[p. 3]
One morning Bobby Bear
said he could not play.
Bobby said, "I have to go
to the doctor today."

Turn the page.

[p. 5]
Pablo Porcupine said,
"You look scared, Bobby Bear."
"I've never been to the doctor," Bobby said.
"I don't know what happens there."

Aroo, aroo. Bobby Bear is scared. Why is Bobby scared? **PAUSE.** Because he doesn't know what will happen at the doctor. Bobby has never been to the doctor, so he is scared to go there.

Turn the page.

[p. 7]
"Don't worry," said Pablo.
"We will all come along."
To help him feel better,
they sang Bobby a song.

Turn the page.

[p. 9]
Bobby had to wait at the doctor,
but he didn't mind.
His friends stayed and played with him.
They were very kind.

Aroo, aroo. Bobby's friends are kind. They do nice things for him. Kind. Say kind. **PAUSE.** Kind means nice. Tell me, what word means nice? **PAUSE.** Kind! Good thinking! What are some nice things you do? **PAUSE.** Maybe you open the door for your teacher, or help your friend clean up, or make a picture for your mom. If you do those things, you are being kind. You are being nice. Now lift the flap. **PAUSE.** Fae is giving her grandma a hug. That's so nice. Fae is kind. Tell me, what does kind mean? **PAUSE.** Nice! Good thinking.

Turn the page.

[p. 10]
"Bobby Bear!" called the doctor.
"You'll be fine. Please sit down."
"I am just a little afraid,"
said Bobby Bear with a frown.

Turn the page.

[p. 13]
Then the tiny doctor said,
"Bobby, open up wide.
I will use this tool
to take a good look inside."

Turn the page.

[p. 15]
When Bobby opened his mouth,
he coughed louder than ever before.
And he blew the tiny doctor
right out of the door!

Turn the page.

[p. 17]
"Now let's see how tall you are,"
the tiny doctor said.
The doctor stacked some chairs
to reach the top of Bobby's head.

Turn the page.

[p. 19]
The doctor was short,
and Bobby Bear was soooo tall.
One bear sneeze—ACHOO—
caused the doctor to fall.

Aroo, aroo. Bobby is so tall! Point to Bobby. Tall. Say tall. **PAUSE.** Now point to the doctor. The doctor is short. Say short. **PAUSE.** Nice job!

Turn the page.

[p. 20]
When the doctor got up,
she said, "I am okay.
Now please step on the scale,
so I can see how much you weigh."

Turn the page.

[p. 23]
But Bobby was so big,
he broke the scale when he tried.
"Oops! I didn't mean to.
It was an accident," he cried.

Aroo, aroo. Bobby did not mean to break the scale! It was an accident. Accident. Say accident. **PAUSE.** Accident means something you didn't mean to do. Tell me, what word means something you didn't mean to do? **PAUSE.** Accident. Great job!

One time, I bumped into my friend and she fell down. I didn't mean to. It was an accident. Now lift the flap. **PAUSE.** Uh-oh. Someone spilled a glass of milk. It was an accident. Say, "Oops!" **PAUSE.** Tell me, what does accident mean? **PAUSE.** Something you didn't mean to do. Great thinking!

Turn the page.

[p. 24]
Bobby Bear felt so embarrassed
that he started to cry.
The doctor said, "It's alright, Bobby.
There's something else we can try."

Turn the page.

[p. 26]
"Just hold this under your tongue
for a minute or two.
Great job! I knew there was
something we could do."

Turn the page.

[p. 28]
"We are all done now," said the doctor.
"Would you like a balloon?
You can share it with your friends
when you see them very soon."

Turn the page.

[p. 31]
On the way home, Fae Fox said,
"I like your balloon, Bobby Bear.
I can't wait to visit the doctor.
It was really fun there."

Turn the page.

[p. 33]
"Oh, boy!" said Bobby.
"I want to come, too!
And this time,
I'll sing a song just for you."

Aroo, aroo. Wow! Bobby Bear learned a lot at the doctor. Hmm. I have some questions for you. In this story, the friends went to the doctor with Bobby Bear. Why did they go with him? **PAUSE.** Because they wanted Bobby to feel better. Bobby was scared, and his friends wanted to cheer him up.

Do you think Bobby Bear will be scared the next time he goes to the doctor? **PAUSE.** No, because he learned the doctor isn't scary! The doctor was really nice to Bobby and gave him a balloon. I bet Bobby will be excited to go to the doctor next time!

Turn the page.

Let's talk about the words we learned. Look at the picture of the little boy. He is helping his friend with his work. That's so nice. He is kind. Say kind. **PAUSE.** Tell me, what does kind mean? **PAUSE.** Nice. Great Job!

Now look at the picture of the little girl. Uh-oh. She made such a mess. She didn't mean to. It was an accident! Say accident. **PAUSE.** Tell me, what does accident mean? **PAUSE.** Something you didn't mean to do. Great thinking!

Turn the page.

Look at the Forest Friends. Let's see. Is Bobby Bear short or tall? **PAUSE.** Tall! Bobby Bear is tall! Is Suki Squirrel short or tall? **PAUSE.** Short! Suki is short! Great work!

I had so much fun with you at the Listening Center today! Thank you for coming. Raise your hand so your teacher knows you are finished. See you tomorrow!

Unit 4 Review, Week 18

Suki Squirrel Goes Swimming

Vocabulary Review: agree, terrified, kind, accident, protect, disappointed

Aroo, aroo. Hello again! Welcome to the Listening Center. It's me, Wanda the Word Wolf. Remember, when you hear me say *Aroo, aroo,* it means it is time for you to answer some questions.

Do you have your book? **PAUSE.** Make sure it is closed, and do not open it until I tell you to. Look at the front cover of your book. Do you see a picture of Suki Squirrel on the cover? **PAUSE.** Yes! Now put your finger under the first word of the title. Follow the arrow under the words as we read the title of the book together. It says, *Suki Squirrel Goes Swimming.*

Go ahead and open your book now.

Turn the page.

[p. 2]
It was a hot and sunny day in the forest.
The Forest Friends wanted to cool down.

Turn the page.

[p. 4]
"Let's go to the pool!" said Fae Fox.
"Yes!" said Bobby Bear and Pablo Porcupine.
They both agreed that swimming
would be a great way to cool down.

Aroo, aroo. Bobby and Pablo agreed to go swimming. They said yes! Agree. Say agree. **PAUSE.** Agree means to say yes. Tell me, what does agree mean? **PAUSE.** To say yes. You got it!

Turn the page.

[p. 7]
But Suki Squirrel was very quiet.
She frowned and didn't say a word.
Suki's friends asked her what was wrong.

Turn the page.

[p. 8]
"I am terrified of water," Suki said.
"I am really scared to go swimming!"

Aroo, aroo. Look at Suki Squirrel. She is really scared of the water. She is terrified! Say terrified. **PAUSE.** Terrified means really scared. Tell me, what does terrified mean? **PAUSE.** Really scared. That's right!

Turn the page.

[p. 10]
"Don't worry," said Pablo Porcupine.
"You don't have to get in the water.
You can sit by the pool or float on a raft instead.
It will still be lots of fun!"

Turn the page.

[p. 12]
Suki decided she would give it a try.
Maybe the pool would not be so scary
if all of her friends were there.

Turn the page.

[p. 14]
When the Forest Friends got to the pool,
they laid their towels out on the grass.
Bobby and Fae were so excited to swim.
They ran straight to the pool and jumped in the water.

Turn the page.

[p. 16]
Pablo Porcupine knew Suki was afraid,
so he sat by the pool with her.
They splashed their feet in the cool water.
Pablo was kind.
It was nice of him to stay with Suki.

Aroo, aroo. Pablo is being nice to Suki Squirrel. He is being kind! Say kind. **PAUSE.** Kind means nice. Tell me, what does kind mean? **PAUSE.** Nice. Great job!

Turn the page.

[p. 19]
Then Bobby Bear swam up to them.
"Do you want to float on my raft?" he asked.
"Sure!" Suki Squirrel said.
She wasn't scared as long as
she didn't have to get in the water.

Turn the page.

[p. 20]
"Come on, Pablo!" said Suki happily.
But when Pablo Porcupine sat down,
his pointy quills made a hole in the raft.
"I didn't mean to," Pablo said. "It was an accident!"

Aroo, aroo. Oh, no! Pablo made a hole in the raft. He didn't mean to do it; it was an accident. Say accident. **PAUSE.** Accident means something you didn't mean to do. Tell me, what does accident mean? **PAUSE.** Something you didn't mean to do. Good thinking!

Turn the page.

[p. 22]
All the air started to leak out of the raft.
Pablo jumped into the water,
but Suki Squirrel was too scared.
"Uh-oh," Suki cried. "I don't know how to swim!"

Turn the page.

[p. 24]
"It's okay," Bobby Bear said.
"I will protect you. I will keep you safe."
Bobby held Suki's hand so she didn't go underwater.

Aroo, aroo. Bobby is keeping Suki safe in the water. He is protecting her! Protect. Say protect. **PAUSE.** Protect means to keep someone safe. Tell me, what does protect mean? **PAUSE.** To keep someone safe. Good job!

Turn the page.

[p. 26]
Then all the friends joined hands
and swam around the pool.
Suki Squirrel felt safe with her friends helping her.
"Wheeee!" Suki shouted. "Swimming is fun!"

Turn the page.

[p. 29]
Just then it started to rain.
The lifeguard blew his whistle,
and everyone had to get out of the pool.

Turn the page.

[p. 30]
The Forest Friends were sad
that they couldn't swim anymore.
They were really disappointed.

Aroo, aroo. Look at the friends. They are sad. They are disappointed. Say disappointed. **PAUSE.** Disappointed means sad. Tell me, what does disappointed mean? **PAUSE.** Sad. Nice work!

Turn the page.

[p. 32]
"Aw," said Suki. "I was having so much fun.
I am not scared of the water anymore!
Can we come back and swim tomorrow?"

Turn the page.

[p. 34]
"Of course," said Fae Fox.
"The pool is the best way to stay cool
on a hot summer day."

I had a lot of fun with you in the Listening Center today! Thank you for coming! Raise your hand so your teacher knows you are finished. See you tomorrow!

Unit 5, Week 19

Fae's Nose Knows

Vocabulary: lost, worried
Concept Words: near, far

Aroo, aroo. Hello again. Welcome to the Listening Center. It's me, Wanda the Word Wolf. Do you have your book? **PAUSE.** Do you see a picture of Fae Fox on the cover? **PAUSE.** Yes! Now put your finger under the first word of the title. Follow the arrow under the words as we read the title of the book together. It says, *Fae's Nose Knows.*

Go ahead and open your book now.

Turn the page.

[p. 2]
Bobby, Suki, and Pablo
met Fae Fox in the forest to play.
"Remember," Fae said,
"we're visiting my grandmother today."

Turn the page.

[p. 5]
Fae said, "Grandmother is baking
fresh homemade pies.
The flavor is a secret,
a tasty surprise!"

Turn the page.

[p. 6]
Grandmother's den was near.
It was not far away.
But on the way there,
the friends started to play.

Aroo, aroo. The Forest Friends are on their way to grandmother's house. Look at the picture of the Forest Friends. Put your finger on Fae Fox. Fae is near. Say near. **PAUSE.** Now put your finger on Pablo Porcupine. Pablo is far! Say far. **PAUSE.** Good work!

Turn the page.

[p. 8]
First, they played tag
and then Hide and Seek.
Soon they came to a place
that was strange and unique.

Turn the page.

[p. 13]
"Oh, no!" cried Fae Fox.
"We don't know where we are!
I think that we are lost.
I wonder if we've gone too far?"

Aroo, aroo. Oh, no! The friends are lost. They don't know where they are. Lost. Say lost. **PAUSE.** Lost means you don't know where you are. Tell me, what word means you don't know where you are? **PAUSE.** Lost! Good thinking! One time I was lost at the mall. I went the wrong way and I didn't know where I was. Has that ever happened to you? **PAUSE.** Now, lift the flap to see Suki. **PAUSE.** She is lost! She does not know where she is. Help her find her way to Bobby. Put your finger on Suki and follow the path to Bobby. Yay! Suki is not lost anymore. Tell me, what does lost mean? **PAUSE.** You don't know where you are. Good thinking!

Turn the page.

[p. 12]
The friends searched and searched
for Grandmother's den,
but they kept ending up
at the same place again.

Turn the page.

[p. 15]
"I hope Grandmother isn't too worried,"
Fae thought.
"Sometimes Grandmother
does worry a lot."

Aroo, aroo. Look at the picture of Fae's grandma. She is worried. She is scared something bad might happen. Worried. Say worried. **PAUSE.** Worried means scared something bad might happen. What word means scared something bad might happen? **PAUSE.** Worried. Great thinking! If your friend doesn't come to school, you might be worried about them. You might be scared something bad happened to your friend. Now lift the flap. **PAUSE.** This boy is worried about his friend. Look at his face. Can you make a worried face? **PAUSE.** Wow! You look scared. Tell me, what does worried mean? **PAUSE.** Scared something bad might happen. That's right.

Turn the page.

[p. 17]
The Forest Friends wondered
if they would ever get there.
Then suddenly Fae's nose
sprung up into the air.

Turn the page.

[p. 19]
Fae said, "Foxes sure do
have a good sense of smell.
Grandmother's den is very near.
I can tell."

Turn the page.

[p. 20]
The Forest Friends marched
with their noses held high.
They followed the scent
of fresh, homemade pie.

Turn the page.

[p. 23]
A few minutes later,
Grandmother's den was in sight.
The friends ran together
as the day turned to night.

Turn the page.

[p. 24]
"We are sorry we're late, Grandmother!"
said Fae.
"We started to play games
and got lost on the way."

Turn the page.

[p. 26]
"That's all right," said Grandmother
with a friendly fox smile.
"You are safe now,
but I was worried for a while."

Aroo, aroo. Fae's grandma is happy. Why is she happy? **PAUSE.** Because Fae and her friends are safe. They finally got to Grandma's house.

Turn the page.

[p. 29]
Grandmother said, "If you like pies
made with blueberry, cherry, apple, or peach,
then you are in luck
because I baked one of each!"

Turn the page.

[p. 30]
So each of the friends
got a whole pie to eat.
Grandmother's pies were delicious.
What a treat!

Aroo, aroo. Wow! That was a fun story! I'm so glad the Forest Friends found Grandmother's den. Hmm. I have some questions for you. When the friends got to the den, Fae Fox told her grandmother she was sorry. Why did Fae say she was sorry? **PAUSE.** Because her grandma was worried about her! Fae and her friends were late because they played in the woods! Fae felt bad that her grandma was worried.

Do you think the Forest Friends will visit Fae's grandma again? **PAUSE.** Yes! Because they had a good time at Fae's grandma's house. Fae's grandma was really nice to them, and she made them some pies. They will probably want to visit again.

Turn the page.

Let's talk about the words we learned. Look at the picture of Bobby Bear. He doesn't know where he is! He is lost. Say lost. **PAUSE.** Tell me, what does lost mean? **PAUSE.** You don't know where you are!

Look at this little boy. He left his favorite toy outside. Now he is scared something bad might happen to it. He is worried. Say worried. **PAUSE.** Tell me, what does worried mean? **PAUSE.** Scared something bad might happen. Nice work!

Turn the page.

Look at the picture of the Forest Friends playing by the tree. Now can you find Grandmother's den in the picture? Are the friends near or far from the den? **PAUSE.** Far! Way to go!

Now look at the Forest Friends chasing each other. Are they near or far from the den? **PAUSE.** Near. Great thinking!

I had so much fun with you at the Listening Center today! Thank you for coming. Raise your hand so your teacher knows you are finished. See you tomorrow!

Unit 5, Week 20

Snow Day for Fae

Vocabulary: complete, frosty
Concept Words: bottom, top

Aroo, aroo. Hello again. Welcome to the listening center. It's me, Wanda the Word Wolf. Do you have your book? **PAUSE.** Do you see a picture of a Snow Fox on the cover? **PAUSE.** Yes! Now put your finger under the first word of the title. Follow the arrow under the words as we read the title of the book together. It says, *Snow Day for Fae.*

Go ahead and open your book now.

In this story, Fae and her friends have a snow day! A snow day is when you stay home from school because there is so much snow on the ground. On a snow day, you can go outside and play in the snow! That sounds like a lot of fun!

Turn the page.

[p. 2]
Fae Fox was waking up
when she heard her mother say,
"Today is a snow day.
You can go outside and play!"

Turn the page.

[p. 5]
"School is closed," Mother said,
"and your friends are outside."
"I can't wait to play in the snow!"
Fae replied.

Aroo, aroo. School is closed, so Fae Fox is going to play outside. What do you like to do when school is closed? **PAUSE.** I like to stay in my pajamas and play with my toys. Sometimes I read books, too.

Turn the page.

[p. 7]
Mother said, "It snowed and snowed
all through the night."
When Fae looked out the window,
she saw quite a sight.

Turn the page.

[p. 9]
Pablo Porcupine, Suki Squirrel,
and Bobby Bear all were there.
"Look, Fae!" they shouted.
"The snow is EVERYWHERE!"

Turn the page.

[p. 11]
Fae had an idea.
"Hey, Suki, I know!
Let's build some Forest Friends
out of the snow!"

Turn the page.

[p. 13]
They built a snow fox, a snow bear,
and a snow squirrel that looked neat.
When they finished the porcupine,
their snow friends were complete!

Aroo, aroo. Point to the picture of the snow friends. They are complete! They are all done. Complete. Say complete. **PAUSE.** Complete means all done! Tell me, what word means all done? **PAUSE.** Complete. Good work! Do you like to put puzzles together? **PAUSE.** When you put the last piece in your puzzle, your puzzle is complete. It's all done! Now put your finger on the flap. Don't open it yet! See the pieces of the snow friend? I see a scarf and some snowballs. Can you help build the snow friend? Lift the flap! **PAUSE.** Look, the snow friend is complete. It is all done! Tell me, what does complete mean? **PAUSE.** All done. Nice job!

Turn the page.

[p. 14]
After the snow friends were done,
Bobby Bear got his sled.
"Let's walk up that hill and race down!" Bobby said.

Turn the page.

[p. 17]
Racing down the hill
sure sounded like fun.
But Bobby's sled did not
have room for everyone.

Turn the page.

[p. 18]
So Fae sat in front,
and Bobby helped Pablo climb.
They would all squeeze on the sled
just this one time.

Turn the page.

[p. 20]
"Faster... faster!
We're flying!" yelled Fae.
The snow friends they built
were still far away.

Aroo, aroo. Look at this silly picture! Put your finger on Suki. Suki is on top of Bobby! Top. Say top. **PAUSE.** Now put your finger on Bobby. He is on the bottom. Say bottom. **PAUSE.** Great work!

Turn the page.

[p. 21]
But the sled was too small
and too hard to steer.
They were heading right for
the snow friends! Oh, dear!

Turn the page.

[p. 25]
And then . . . KABOOM!!!
After racing so fast,
the Forest Friends crashed
into the snow friends at last.

Turn the page.

[p. 26]
"It's frosty!" yelled Fae.
"I'm covered in snow.
It's too cold to play.
I think we should go."

Aroo, aroo. Look at the Forest Friends outside in the snow. It is frosty. It is really cold. Frosty. Say frosty. **PAUSE.** Frosty means cold. Tell me, what word means cold? **PAUSE.** Frosty! Good work! In the winter, it is cold outside. When there is snow on the ground and the sidewalk is icy, it is frosty. It is cold! Pretend you are outside and it is frosty. Shiver and rub your arms. Say Brr, it's frosty! Tell me, what does frosty mean? **PAUSE.** Cold. Great thinking!

Turn the page.

[p. 28]
The next day it was warmer
when the friends went out to play,
and the hot sun had melted
all of the snow away.

Turn the page.

[p. 30]
The friends would have to wait
until the snow came again.
But there were lots of other games
they could play until then.

Aroo, aroo. The friends sure had a lot of fun playing in the snow! Hmm. I have some questions for you. At the beginning of the story, Fae's friends were waiting at her house. Why were her friends waiting for her? **PAUSE.** Because they wanted to play with her! It was snowy outside and they thought it would be fun to play together.

The next time it snows, do you think the Forest Friends will sled down the big hill again? **PAUSE.** Yes, because it was fun to go so fast! They felt like they were flying. I bet they will want to do it again.

Turn the page.

Let's talk about the words we learned. Look at the picture of the blocks. Point to the tower made of blocks. The tower is all done. It is complete. Say complete. **PAUSE.** Tell me, what does complete mean? **PAUSE.** All done. Great work!

Now look at the little boy in the snow. He is wearing a warm coat because it is cold outside. It is frosty. Say frosty. **PAUSE.** Tell me, what does frosty mean? **PAUSE.** Cold. Nice job!

Turn the page.

Look at the picture of the hill. Put your finger on Suki. Is Suki at the top of the hill or at the bottom of the hill? **PAUSE.** The bottom! Suki is at the bottom of the hill!

Now put your finger on Bobby. Is Bobby at the top of the hill or at the bottom of the hill? **PAUSE.** The top! Bobby is at the top of the hill. Awesome!

I had so much fun with you at the Listening Center today! Thank you for coming. Raise your hand so your teacher knows you are finished. See you tomorrow!

Unit 5, Week 21

Where Is Bobby Bear?

Vocabulary: exhausted, search
Concept Words: winter, spring

Aroo, aroo. Hello again. Welcome to the Listening Center. It's me, Wanda the Word Wolf. Do you have your book? **PAUSE.** Do you see a picture of Fae Fox and Suki Squirrel on the cover? **PAUSE.** Yes! Now put your finger under the first word of the title. Follow the arrow under the words as we read the title of the book together. It says, *Where Is Bobby Bear?*

Go ahead and open your book now.

Bobby is a bear. Bears do a special thing in the winter. Bears hibernate. They go to sleep for the whole winter. The whole winter! What a long time to sleep. Let's start our story.

Turn the page.

[p. 3]
On the first day of winter,
the ground was snowy and white.
Bobby Bear said,
"Hey! Let's have a snowball fight!"

Turn the page.

[p. 5]
Bobby played with his friends
until the day was done.
Then he said, "I'm tired.
Let's come back tomorrow to have more fun!"

Turn the page.

[p. 6]
When Bobby got home,
he couldn't wait to go to bed.
"Go wash up, and I will tuck you in,"
Mother said.

Turn the page.

[p. 9]
Bobby said, "I'm exhausted,"
as Mother tucked him in tight.
"I'm glad you're really tired," she said.
"We start to hibernate tonight."

Aroo, aroo. Bobby is exhausted. He is really tired. Exhausted. Say exhausted. **PAUSE.** Exhausted means really tired. Tell me, what word means really tired? **PAUSE.** Exhausted. Good work. If you play outside all day, or stay up really late at night, you might be exhausted. You might be really tired. Show me what you do when you are really tired. Yawn and say,

"I'm exhausted." **PAUSE.** Tell me, what does exhausted mean? **PAUSE.** Really tired. Great thinking!

Turn the page.

[p. 11]
The next day Suki, Fae, and Pablo
met at their special tree.
Everyone was there except Bobby Bear.
Where could he be?

Turn the page.

[p. 12]
The Forest Friends waited,
and then they started to worry.
They decided to look for Bobby
and ran to his house in a hurry.

Aroo, aroo. Pablo, Fae, and Suki are looking everywhere for Bobby Bear. Why are they looking for Bobby? **PAUSE.** Because they are worried about their friend. Bobby didn't come to the tree, and they don't know where he is.

Turn the page.

[p. 15]
The friends tapped on the door
quietly at first.
Then they banged so loud
that the door nearly burst!

Turn the page.

[p. 17]
"No one answered," said Suki.
"Where is Bobby Bear?"
Fae said, "What if he is lost
in the forest somewhere?"

Turn the page.

[p. 18]
The friends searched in the woods,
down a hillside and more.
They called out Bobby's name,
but they heard no bear roar!

Aroo, aroo. The Forest Friends searched for Bobby. They looked for Bobby everywhere! Search. Say search. **PAUSE.** Search means to look for something. Tell me, what word means to look for something? **PAUSE.** Search! Good work. Do you ever have to search for a toy you can't find? **PAUSE.** You might look under your bed and in your closet. Now, lift the flap. **PAUSE.** Look at all the animals! Can you search for the rabbit? **PAUSE.** Look at each picture to see if you can find it. You are searching! Great work! Tell me, what does search mean? **PAUSE.** To look for something. Awesome job!

Turn the page.

[p. 20]
The friends didn't know
where else to look for Bobby Bear.
Then a blue jay called down
from high up in the air.

Turn the page.

[p. 23]
"I think I can help you
find your lost friend.
He will return in the spring,
when winter comes to an end."

Turn the page.

[p. 24]
"Your friend will wake up
when the sun melts the snow,
the grass turns green,
and the flowers start to grow."

Aroo, aroo. The blue jay says Bobby will wake up in the spring. Say spring. **PAUSE.** In the spring, the grass turns green and the leaves grow on the trees. Bobby sleeps in the winter. Say winter. **PAUSE.** In the winter, it is cold and there can be snow on the ground. Let's see what happens next.

Turn the page.

[p. 27]
"Bears hibernate!
They sleep the whole winter through!
In the spring, Bobby Bear
will wake up and play with you!"

Turn the page.

[p. 29]
The friends waited and waited
until the winter had passed.
Then spring finally came.
Would they see Bobby Bear at last?

Turn the page.

[p. 30]
Pablo, Fae, and Suki
ran to their special tree.
Bobby Bear was waiting there,
just as he said he would be.

Aroo, aroo. I'm so glad Bobby Bear woke up and met his friends at their special tree. Hmm. I have some questions for you. What did the Forest Friends learn from the bird? **PAUSE.** They learned that bears sleep in the winter. The bird told them they would have to wait for Bobby Bear to wake up in the spring.

At the end of the story, the friends were happy. Why were the friends happy? **PAUSE.** Because Bobby Bear came back! Bobby woke up and met them at their special tree! I bet they missed him and were happy to see him again.

Turn the page.

Let's talk about the words we learned. Look at the little girl sitting at the table. I think she needs a nap. She is really tired. She is exhausted. Say exhausted. **PAUSE.** Tell me, what does exhausted mean? **PAUSE.** Really tired. Great job!

Now look at the little girl with the curly hair. She lost her dog at the park and she is looking everywhere for him. She is searching. Search. Say search. **PAUSE.** Tell me, what does search mean? **PAUSE.** To look for something. Great thinking!

Turn the page.

Point to the picture where there is snow on the ground. Is it winter or spring? **PAUSE.** Winter. Good thinking!

Now, point to the picture where the trees have leaves. Is it winter or spring? **PAUSE.** Spring. Awesome job!

I had so much fun with you at the Listening Center today! Thank you for coming. Raise your hand so your teacher knows you are finished. See you tomorrow!

Unit 5 Review, Week 22

Pablo Packs a Picnic

Vocabulary Review: complete, search, lost, worried, frosty, exhausted

Aroo, aroo. Hello again! Welcome to the Listening Center. It's me, Wanda the Word Wolf. Remember, when you hear me say *Aroo, aroo,* it means it is time for you to answer some questions.

Do you have your book? **PAUSE.** Make sure it is closed, and do not open it until I tell you to. Look at the front cover of your book. Do you see a picture of Pablo Porcupine on the cover? **PAUSE.** Yes! Now put your finger under the first word of the title. Follow the arrow under the words as we read the title of the book together. It says, *Pablo Packs a Picnic.*

Go ahead and open your book now.

Turn the page.

[p. 3]
One morning, Pablo Porcupine
asked his friends to go on a picnic.
They would eat lunch in the woods
by their favorite tree.

Turn the page.

[p. 4]
Pablo's job was to pack the lunch.
First, he made peanut butter and jelly sandwiches.
He carefully placed the sandwiches in a picnic basket.

Turn the page.

[p. 7]
Next, Pablo packed snacks and drinks.
He put apples, crackers, and juice in the picnic basket.

Turn the page.

[p. 9]
Finally, Pablo packed a surprise treat.
He put ice cream in the picnic basket
and hoped it would not melt.
Now Pablo's job was complete.
He was all done packing for the picnic.

Aroo, aroo. Look! Pablo is done packing the lunch. His job is complete.

Say complete. **PAUSE.** Complete means all done. Tell me, what does complete mean? **PAUSE.** All done. That's right!

Turn the page.

[p. 11]
The Forest Friends were so excited for the picnic!
They gathered a blanket and Pablo's basket
and walked into the woods.
They just needed to find their favorite tree.

Turn the page.

[p. 13]
The friends knew their favorite tree
was on a hill covered with pretty flowers.
They looked all around, but they did not see a hill
and they did not see any flowers.
They kept searching for their special tree.

Aroo, aroo. The friends are looking for their favorite tree. They are searching for it! Search. Say search. **PAUSE.** Search means to look for something. Tell me, what does search mean? **PAUSE.** To look for something! Nice job.

Turn the page.

[p. 14]
"Where is our favorite tree?" cried Suki Squirrel.
The friends were getting hungry.
They needed to find their special picnic spot,
but it was nowhere to be seen.

Turn the page.

[p. 17]
The Forest Friends realized they were lost.
They did not know where they were.

Aroo, aroo. Look at the Forest Friends. They don't know where they are! They are lost! Say lost. **PAUSE.** Lost means you don't know where you are. Tell me, what does lost mean? **PAUSE.** You don't know where you are. Good work!

Turn the page.

[p. 19]
"Hmm. I think I smell flowers," said Fae Fox.
She pointed down a path.
"Let's go that way."
The Forest Friends walked quickly behind Fae.

Turn the page.

[p. 20]
"I hope this is the right way," Pablo Porcupine thought.
Pablo was worried.
He was afraid the ice cream would melt if they didn't have their picnic soon.
Then his surprise treat would be ruined.

Aroo, aroo. Look at Pablo. He is scared his ice cream might melt. He is worried. Say worried. **PAUSE.** Worried means scared something bad might happen. Tell me, what does worried mean? **PAUSE.** Scared something bad might happen. Great thinking!

Turn the page.

[p. 23]
All of a sudden, the friends came
to the bottom of a hill.
They saw pretty flowers
and knew their favorite tree was nearby.

Turn the page.

[p. 24]
"Yippee!" Fae Fox shouted.
"I see our special tree!"
Fae and her friends ran to the tree
and laid out the picnic blanket beneath it.

Turn the page.

[p. 27]
"The friends opened up the picnic basket
and started eating their lunch.
They were very hungry,
so they ate all the sandwiches, apples, and crackers.

Turn the page.

[p. 28]
Finally, it was time for Pablo's surprise treat.
Pablo gave each friend
a bowl of frosty ice cream.
It was still cold, and it was very tasty!

Aroo, aroo. Yay! Pablo's ice cream is still cold. It is frosty! Say frosty. **PAUSE.** Frosty means cold. Tell me, what does frosty mean? **PAUSE.** Cold. You got it!

Turn the page.

[p. 31]
When the Forest Friends had finished their lunch,
they played a game of tag.
They ran around under their tree and all over the hillside.

Turn the page.

[p. 33]
After playing tag, the friends were very tired.
They had been walking and running
around the forest all morning.
They were exhausted.

Aroo, aroo. Phew! The Forest Friends are really tired. They are exhausted. Say exhausted. **PAUSE.** Exhausted means really tired. Tell me, what does exhausted mean? **PAUSE.** Really tired. Alright!

Turn the page.

[p. 35]
The friends snuggled up under their special tree.
The picnic was a lot of fun, but now they needed a nap.
The friends closed their eyes and quietly fell asleep.

I had a lot of fun with you in the Listening Center today! Thank you for coming! Raise your hand so your teacher knows you are finished. See you tomorrow!

Unit 6, Week 23

Pablo's Map Matters

Vocabulary: thrilled, ignore
Concept Words: quiet, loud

Aroo, aroo. Hello again. Welcome to the Listening Center. It's me, Wanda the Word Wolf. Do you have your book? **PAUSE.** Do you see a picture of Pablo Porcupine on the cover? **PAUSE.** Yes! Now put your finger under the first word of the title. Follow the arrow under the words as we read the title of the book together. It says, *Pablo's Map Matters.*

Go ahead and open your book now.

In this book, the Forest Friends are going to a carnival. A carnival is like a circus. At a carnival, there are games and rides. Have you ever been to a carnival? **PAUSE.** They are lots of fun. Let's start the story.

Turn the page.

[p. 3]
One day Pablo Porcupine
met his friends at their special tree.
He was going to spend the day
with Bobby, Fae, and Suki.

Turn the page.

[p. 5]
The friends were all going
to a carnival today,
and Pablo had a map
to help them find the way.

Turn the page.

[p. 6]
The Forest Friends were thrilled!
Bobby let out a mighty roar!
Fae Fox ran in circles
on the forest floor.

Aroo, aroo. The Forest Friends are thrilled! They are excited to go to the carnival. Thrilled. Say thrilled. **PAUSE.** Thrilled means excited. Tell me, what word means excited? **PAUSE.** Thrilled. Good work! When are you thrilled? **PAUSE.** What about when you get a present! Or your friends come over to play! I bet that makes you feel excited. Now, lift the flap. **PAUSE.** Look! These boys are at a birthday party. They are excited. They are thrilled! Tell me, what does thrilled mean? **PAUSE.** Excited! That's right.

Turn the page.

[p. 8]
Suki Squirrel jumped around
from tree to tree.
But Pablo was different.
He stood as quiet as could be.

Turn the page.

[p. 11]
"Let's go!" yelled Fae.
"The carnival will soon begin!"
"We have to get there," said Bobby Bear,
"and buy our tickets to get in."

Turn the page.

[p. 13]
To get to the carnival on time,
the Forest Friends had to hurry.
His friends said they knew the way,
so Pablo did not worry.

Turn the page.

[p. 14]
The friends ran down the path
until it split in two.
But Bobby, Suki, and Fae did not know the way.
They did not know what to do.

Turn the page.

[p. 16]
Quiet Pablo was happy.
He brought a map with him today!
He could look at the map
to help them find the way!

Aroo, aroo. Pablo Porcupine brought a map with him. Why did Pablo bring a map? **PAUSE.** Because he wanted to help his friends get to the carnival. Pablo didn't want them to be lost.

Turn the page.

[p. 19]
"Uh-oh!" shouted Suki.
"Which way should we go?"
"That way," said Pablo softly.
"I have a map. I know."

Turn the page.

[p. 21]
But Suki, Fae, and Bobby
did not listen to what Pablo had to say.
Pablo's friends ignored him,
and they marched the other way!

Aroo, aroo. Pablo's friends ignored him. They did not listen. Ignore. Say ignore. **PAUSE.** Ignore means to not listen. Tell me, what word means to not listen? **PAUSE.** Ignore. Good work! If your teacher tells you to clean up and you don't do it, you ignored your teacher. You did not listen. Look at the picture of the Forest Friends. Suki, Fae, and Bobby are going the wrong way! Tell them to turn around! Turn around! Uh-oh, they didn't turn around. They ignored you. They did not listen. Tell me, what does ignore mean? **PAUSE.** To not listen. Great thinking!

Turn the page.

[p. 23]
Pablo followed his friends, and then
the path again split in two.
NOW which way to go?
They did not know what to do.

Turn the page.

[p. 24]
"Hmph!" grunted Bobby Bear.
"Which way should we go?"
"That way," Pablo pointed.
"I have a map. I know."

Turn the page.

[p. 26]
But Suki, Fae, and Bobby
marched the other way.
They still did not listen
to what Pablo had to say.

Turn the page.

[p. 29]
So this time Pablo shouted,
"WAIT! I KNOW WHICH WAY TO GO!
THAT IS THE WAY TO THE CARNIVAL!
I HAVE A MAP. I KNOW!"

Aroo, aroo. Wow! Pablo is shouting. He is loud. Say loud. **PAUSE.** Before, Pablo was talking quietly. He used a quiet voice. Quiet. Say quiet. **PAUSE.** His friends did not listen when Pablo was quiet. Let's see if they listen to his loud voice!

Turn the page.

[p. 31]
Pablo's friends were surprised
to hear him use such a loud voice.
If they had listened to him before,
they would have made the right choice.

Turn the page.

[p. 33]
Pablo's friends followed him
the rest of the way,
and they learned that quiet friends
can have important things to say.

Aroo, aroo. Hooray! I bet the Forest Friends will have a great time at the carnival. Hmm. I have some questions for you. At the end of the story, the friends finally listened to Pablo Porcupine. Why should you listen to your friends? **PAUSE.** Because your friends have important things to say! Pablo wanted to tell his friends something important. If you don't listen to your friends, that will make them feel bad.

Do you think Pablo Porcupine's friends will listen to him the next time they play together? **PAUSE.** Yes, because they learned that Pablo could help them! Pablo was quiet, but he knew how to get to the carnival. I bet they'll listen to Pablo from now on!

Turn the page.

Let's talk about the words we learned. Look at the boys with the soccer ball. They just won their soccer game. They are so excited that they won. They are thrilled! Say thrilled. **PAUSE.** Tell me, what does thrilled mean? **PAUSE.** Excited. Great work!

Look at the picture of Bobby napping. If your friends bother you during naptime, you can not listen to them. You can ignore them. Say ignore. **PAUSE.** Tell me, what does ignore mean? **PAUSE.** To not listen. Nice thinking!

Turn the page.

Look at Pablo talking. Listen to Pablo telling his friends that he knows the way. "That way! I have a map. I know." Tell me, did you hear Pablo speak in a loud voice or a quiet voice? **PAUSE.** Quiet. Good job!

Now look at Pablo shouting. Listen to Pablo again. "WAIT! I KNOW WHICH WAY TO GO! THAT IS THE WAY TO THE CARNIVAL! I HAVE A MAP. I KNOW!" Tell me, did you hear Pablo speak in a loud voice or a quiet voice? **PAUSE.** Loud. Awesome!

I had so much fun with you at the Listening Center today! Thank you for coming. Raise your hand so your teacher knows you are finished. See you tomorrow!

Unit 6, Week 24

Fae's Smelly Situation

Vocabulary: horrible, fail
Concept Words: in, out

Aroo, aroo. Hello again. Welcome to the Listening Center. It's me, Wanda the Word Wolf. Do you have your book? **PAUSE.** Do you see a picture of Fae Fox on the cover? **PAUSE.** Yes! Now put your finger under the first word of the title. Follow the arrow under the words as we read the title of the book together. It says, *Fae's Smelly Situation.*

Go ahead and open your book now.

Here is a picture of an animal with black and white fur. It is called a skunk, and it can do something special. When a skunk is scared, it sprays a yucky smell so other animals will run away. In this story, Fae Fox is going to find a skunk! Let's see what happens.

Turn the page.

[p. 3]
Fae Fox woke up
and got ready to play.
She was meeting her friends
in the forest today.

Turn the page.

[p. 5]
As Fae walked along
the forest trail,
she saw something strange—
a mysterious tail.

Turn the page.

[p. 7]
Fae wondered what it was
so she grabbed the tail to see
just what kind of creature
this creature could be.

Turn the page.

[p. 9]
"Oh, no!" cried Fae.
"This tail belongs to a skunk!"
Then the skunk sprayed Fae
with a yucky, smelly funk!

Turn the page.

[p. 10]
Now Fae was so smelly
she needed help from her friends.
She ran to find them
where the long trail ends.

Turn the page.

[p. 13]
"Eww, you stink!" cried Pablo Porcupine,
Suki Squirrel, and Bobby Bear.
"We've never smelled a smell
so horrible anywhere!"

Aroo, aroo. Fae Fox smells horrible. She smells really bad. Horrible. Say horrible. **PAUSE.** Horrible means really bad. Tell me, what word means really bad? **PAUSE.** Horrible. That's right! Can you think of some other things that smell horrible? **PAUSE.** What about stinky shoes? Or a wet dog? Now lift the flap to see something else that smells horrible. **PAUSE.** Ewww, trash! Trash smells really bad. Say that's horrible! **PAUSE.** Tell me, what does horrible mean? **PAUSE.** Really bad. Good thinking!

Turn the page.

[p. 15]
Fae's friends pinned their noses
to make the smell go away.
Then Pablo got an idea
to help his stinky friend Fae.

Turn the page.

[p. 16]
"If we rub berries on you," said Pablo,
"then you will smell sweet."
But Fae learned that berries
are only good to eat.

Turn the page.

[p. 19]
The pins came off their noses,
and the friends inhaled.
It was soon very clear
that the berries had failed.

Aroo, aroo. Oh, no! Fae is still smelly! The berries failed. They did not work. Fail. Say fail. **PAUSE.** Fail means to not work. Tell me, what word means to not work? **PAUSE.** Fail. Great thinking!

Now, listen carefully. If you wanted to cut some paper, would you use a spoon? **PAUSE.** No! A spoon would not work. A spoon would fail. Would you use a crayon to cut paper? **PAUSE.** No! A crayon would not cut paper. It would fail. Hmm. I have an idea. Let's try to touch the ceiling. Reach your arms way up high! Did you touch the ceiling? **PAUSE.** Not me. I failed. It did not work. Tell me, what does fail mean? **PAUSE.** To not work. Nice job!

Turn the page.

[p. 20]
"Eww, you stink!" they cried.
"And now you're purple, too!"
But Bobby Bear had an idea
of what Fae could do.

Turn the page.

[p. 22]
"Gather some leaves," said Bobby,
"and we'll put them to use."
Fae rolled in the leaves
to clean off the smell and the juice."

Turn the page.

[p. 25]
But did the leaves work?
No, they did not.
"What can I do?"
poor Fae Fox thought.

Aroo, aroo. Fae Fox is sad. Why is Fae sad? **PAUSE.** Because she is still smelly and dirty. Bobby Bear's idea did not work.

Turn the page.

[p. 27]
"Eww, you stink!" cried the friends.
"And now you're dirty, too!"
But Suki Squirrel had an idea
of what Fae could do.

Turn the page.

[p. 29]
"Try this flower necklace," said Suki.
"I made it just for you.
It will make you look pretty
and smell better, too!"

Turn the page.

[p. 31]
Fae put on the necklace
that her friend Suki made,
but she was still purple, dirty, and smelly
... and suddenly very afraid.

Turn the page.

[p. 33]
What buzzes and loves flowers?
Think quickly, please.
They're yellow, and black, and buzzing.
They are...

Turn the page.

[p. 35]
BEES!
A swarm of bees chased the friends
through the forest very fast.
So they jumped into a pond
until the bees had passed.

Aroo, aroo. Look at the friends. Put your finger on Bobby Bear. Bobby is in the water. In. Say in. **PAUSE.** Now put your finger on Fae Fox. Fae Fox is out of the water. Out. Say out. **PAUSE.** Great job!

Turn the page.

[p. 37]
When the friends came out of the water,
they were happy to see
that Fae Fox was clean again.
They all shouted, "Yippee!"

Aroo, aroo. Yay! Fae Fox is clean again and not smelly anymore. Hmm. I have some questions for you. In this story, the friends tried to help Fae Fox get clean. Why did they help Fae? **PAUSE.** Because Fae is their friend! Fae was so smelly, she needed help from her friends. If I needed something, my friends would help me, too!

Remember, Fae's friends tried to help her. What can you do to help your friends? **PAUSE.** I can help my friends clean up, or I can help them with their work.

Turn the page.

Let's talk about the words we learned. Look at the picture of the messy bedroom. That mess is really bad! That mess is horrible. Tell me, what does horrible mean? **PAUSE.** Really bad. Good job!

Look at the picture of the pencil. Can you use a pencil to write your name? **PAUSE.** Yes! A pencil would work. Can you use a pencil to brush your teeth? **PAUSE.** No! A pencil would not work. It would fail! Say fail. **PAUSE.** Tell me, what does fail mean? **PAUSE.** To not work. You got it!

Turn the page.

Point to the girl. Is she in the cart or out of the cart? **PAUSE.** In! She is in the cart! Now point to the boy. Is he in the cart or out of the cart? **PAUSE.** Out! He is out of the cart. Nice job!

I had so much fun with you at the Listening Center today! Thank you for coming. Raise your hand so your teacher knows you are finished. See you tomorrow!

Unit 6, Week 25

Suki's Selfish Saturday

Vocabulary: selfish, enjoy
Concept Words: new, old

Aroo, aroo. Hello again. Welcome to the Listening Center. It's me, Wanda the Word Wolf. Do you have your book? **PAUSE.** Do you see a picture of Suki Squirrel on the cover? **PAUSE.** Yes! Now put your finger under the first word of the title. Follow the arrow under the words as we read the title of the book together. It says, *Suki's Selfish Saturday.*

Go ahead and open your book now.

Turn the page.

[p. 3]
Suki Squirrel woke up early
one Saturday.
She was so excited!
Her friends were coming to play!

Turn the page.

[p. 5]
Suki's mom had given her
a brand-new game.
But Suki did not want to share it
with her friends when they came.

Turn the page.

[p. 7]
Suki knew that sharing
was the right thing to do.
But she wanted her game
to stay shiny and new.

Aroo, aroo. Suki Squirrel does not want to share her game. Why doesn't Suki want to share her game? **PAUSE.** Because she's afraid her game will get messed up. Her game is shiny and new, so she doesn't want anyone to play with it.

Turn the page.

[p. 9]
Suki's mom said, "You can play this game
with your friends today."
Selfish Suki said, "This game is mine.
I don't want them to play!"

Aroo, aroo. Suki is selfish. She doesn't want to share her game. Selfish. Say selfish. **PAUSE.** Selfish means you don't want to share. Tell me, what word means you don't want to share? **PAUSE.** Selfish. Good work. Once, I had a big bag of candy and my sister wanted some. But I did not want to share with her. I was selfish. Now, lift the flap. **PAUSE.** Look at Fae. Fae does not want to share her doll. Tell Fae, "That's selfish!" **PAUSE.** Tell me, what does selfish mean? **PAUSE.** You don't want to share. Nice job!

Turn the page.

[p. 11]
When Suki heard her friends
coming to her tree,
she tip-toed to her room
as quietly as could be.

Turn the page.

[p. 12]
Suki hid her new game
under her bed.
Her friends would have to play
with her old toys instead.

Aroo, aroo. Suki hid her new game! Now look at the dolls. Point to the pink doll. The pink doll is new. Say new. **PAUSE.** Now point to the yellow doll. The yellow doll is old. Say old. **PAUSE.** Good work!

Turn the page.

[p. 15]
Then Suki came to the door,
and what did she see?
Each friend had brought
a new toy to her tree.

Turn the page.

[p. 17]
In Suki's room,
Pablo raced a red fire truck,
and Bobby Bear played
with a stuffed yellow duck.

Turn the page.

[p. 19]
Fae Fox danced with a doll
that was pretty and sweet.
Its curly pink hair
smelled like a strawberry treat.

Turn the page.

[p. 20]
Now Suki really hoped
Fae Fox wanted to share,
because Suki wanted to play
with the doll's curly pink hair.

Turn the page.

[p. 23]
So Suki Squirrel asked Fae
if they could trade toys.
Fae said, "No way!
Trade with one of the boys!"

Turn the page.

[p. 24]
But Bobby and Pablo
did not want to share.
Then Suki had an idea
to help them play fair!

Turn the page.

[p. 26]
Suki pulled her new game
from under her bed.
"We would all have more fun
if we shared," Suki said.

Turn the page.

[p. 29]
Fae and Suki played with toys.
Pablo played the game with Bobby Bear.
The friends enjoyed their day.
They were happy to share.

Aroo, aroo. The friends had fun playing together. They enjoyed it. Enjoy. Say enjoy. **PAUSE.** Enjoy means to have fun! Tell me, what word means to have fun? **PAUSE.** Enjoy. Nice job! What are some things that you enjoy? **PAUSE.** What about riding your bike, watching TV, or going to your friend's house? Those are things I enjoy. I have fun doing those things. Now, lift the flap to see something the Forest Friends enjoy. **PAUSE.** Look! They have fun playing soccer. They enjoy it! Tell me, what does enjoy mean? **PAUSE.** To have fun! Good thinking!

Turn the page.

[p. 30]
Suki said goodbye to her friends
after a very fun day.
She had learned that sharing
is the best way to play.

Aroo, aroo. What a great story! Suki had a lot of fun after she decided to share her game. Hmm. I have some questions for you. At the end of the story, the friends shared their toys with each other. Why should you share with your friends? **PAUSE.** Because sharing with your friends will make them happy. Your friends will like playing with your toys, and you will be happy, too!

The next time Suki Squirrel's friends come to her tree, do you think she will share with them? **PAUSE.** Yes, because she learned that it is more fun to share! When Suki shared her new game, her friends shared their toys, too. Suki had more fun when they played together.

Turn the page.

Let's talk about the words we learned. Look at the picture of the girl. She does not want to share her bear with her brother. She is selfish. Say selfish. **PAUSE.** Tell me, what does selfish mean? **PAUSE.** You don't want to share. Awesome!

Look at the little girl in the water. She has fun swimming. She enjoys it. Enjoy. Say enjoy. **PAUSE.** Tell me, what does enjoy mean? **PAUSE.** To have fun. Nice work!

Turn the page.

Look at the shoes. Point to the pink shoes. Are they new or old? **PAUSE.** New! Now point to the other shoes. Are they new or old? **PAUSE.** Old! Great work!

I had so much fun with you at the Listening Center today. Thank you for coming. Raise your hand so your teacher knows you are finished. See you tomorrow!

Unit 6 Review, Week 26

Forest Friends Go to the Library

Vocabulary Review: thrilled, enjoy, ignore, horrible, selfish, fail

Aroo, aroo. Hello again! Welcome to the Listening Center. It's me, Wanda the Word Wolf. Remember, when you hear me say *Aroo, aroo,* it means it is time for you to answer some questions.

Do you have your book? **PAUSE.** Make sure it is closed, and do not open it until I tell you to. Look at the front cover of your book. Do you see a picture of the Forest Friends on the cover? **PAUSE.** Yes! Now put your finger under the first word of the title. Follow the arrow under the words as we read the title of the book together. It says, *Forest Friends Go to the Library.*

Go ahead and open your book now.

Turn the page.

[p. 2]
It was library day at school.
The Forest Friends were thrilled.
Library day was their favorite day of the week.
They were excited to take home some new books!

Aroo, aroo. Look at the friends. They are excited to go to the library. They are thrilled! Say thrilled. **PAUSE.** Thrilled means excited. Tell me, what does thrilled mean? **PAUSE.** Excited. Good thinking!

Turn the page.

[p. 4]
Their teacher told them
they could each check out one new book.
On the way to the library,
the friends thought about the books they would choose.

Turn the page.

[p. 7]
"I really enjoy basketball.
I have fun every time I play," Bobby Bear thought.
Bobby decided he would find a book
about basketball at the library.

Aroo, aroo. Bobby has fun playing basketball. He enjoys it! Enjoy. Say enjoy. **PAUSE.** Enjoy means to have fun. Tell me, what does enjoy mean? **PAUSE.** To havc fun. That's right!

Turn the page.

[p. 9]
When they got to the library, the librarian
asked them to take a seat on the carpet.
"And remember," she said.
"No loud voices in the library."

Turn the page.

[p. 11]
The librarian was going to read the class a story.
The Forest Friends sat beside each other and got ready to listen.
They loved story time.

Turn the page.

[p. 12]
Then Pablo Porcupine whispered, "I'm hungry,"
and asked Suki Squirrel what she brought for lunch.
Suki ignored Pablo.
She knew you shouldn't talk at story time, so she tried not to listen.

Aroo, aroo. Suki is not listening to Pablo. She is ignoring him. Ignore. Say ignore. **PAUSE.** Ignore means to not listen. Tell me, what does ignore mean? **PAUSE.** To not listen. Good job!

Turn the page.

[p. 14]
"Guess what I brought for lunch?" said Pablo.
"A peanut butter and pickle sandwich!"
Suki couldn't keep quict anymore.
"Ewww!" she shouted. "That sounds horrible!"
She thought a peanut butter and pickle sandwich
would taste very bad.

Aroo, aroo. Pablo's lunch sounds really bad. A peanut butter and pickle sandwich sounds horrible! Say horrible. **PAUSE.** Horrible means really bad. Tell me, what does horrible mean? **PAUSE.** Really bad. Nice work!

Turn the page.

[p. 17]
"Shhhhhh!" said the librarian.
"Remember... No loud voices in the library."
Pablo and Suki stayed quiet until story time was over.

Turn the page.

[p. 19]
Then, all the friends got up to look for their books.
Bobby searched the shelves
for a book about basketball.

Turn the page.

[p. 20]
When Bobby found the sports books,
Fae Fox was holding the only book about basketball.
"Can I see that book?" asked Bobby.
But Fae was being selfish.
She didn't want to share the book with Bobby Bear.

Aroo, aroo. Fae Fox doesn't want to share her book. She is being selfish. Say selfish. **PAUSE.** Selfish means you don't want to share. Tell me, what does selfish mean? **PAUSE.** You don't want to share. You got it!

Turn the page.

[p. 22]
Bobby looked sad.
He really wanted a book about basketball.
"I'm sorry," Fae said. "You can check out this book.
I'll get one about soccer, and we can read our books together."

Turn the page.

[p. 24]
Bobby thought that was a great idea.
But the only book about soccer was on the top shelf.
Fae and Bobby could not reach it.

Turn the page.

[p. 27]
"I know," Fae said. "I will stack up these books.
You can stand on them to reach the top shelf."
Bobby stood on the books, but they all fell down.
He still couldn't get the soccer book.
Fae's idea did not work. It failed.

Aroo, aroo. Bobby tried to stand on a stack of books to get the soccer book, but it didn't work. It failed. Fail. Say fail. **PAUSE.** Fail means to not work. Tell me, what does fail mean? **PAUSE.** To not work. Nice job!

Turn the page.

[p. 28]
"Oh, no!" Bobby Bear cried unhappily.
"We'll never reach this book!"
"Shhhhhh!" said the librarian.
"Remember...No loud voices in the library."

Turn the page.

[p. 31]
"Sorry," Bobby said softly.
"Can you help us reach that book?"
The librarian smiled and brought over a ladder.
She took the soccer book from the top shelf and handed it to Bobby.

Turn the page.

[p. 33]
Bobby Bear and Fae Fox quietly thanked the librarian.
Then she helped them check out their books.
The Forest Friends all found books they wanted to borrow.
They could not wait to take them home and read them.

I had a lot of fun with you in the Listening Center today! Thank you for coming! Raise your hand so your teacher knows you are finished. See you tomorrow!

Assessment Contents

Assessment Overview

Universal Screening and Progress Monitoring

Multitiered systems of support (MTSS), also called response to intervention (RTI), are instructional frameworks used to help prevent language and reading difficulties in young children. The primary assessment components of these frameworks are universal screening and progress monitoring. Universal screening for all children identifies those who may need additional support. The screening may have a teacher perception component and an objective testing component. Screening tests are relatively brief assessments and scoring is used to judge whether children pass or fail. If a child passes a screening, there is little concern. Nevertheless, screening is re-administered two or three times during the year.

Monthly progress monitoring that targets areas of concern is recommended for children who fail the screening. Progress monitoring helps determine whether children are catching up to peers and meeting developmental expectations. Many children who exhibit delays in language development will have difficulty catching up to peers without additional explicit instruction. For these children, in MTSS or RTI models, an additional tier of instruction is implemented. Progress monitoring then shows whether the additional tier of instruction is sufficient for the child to catch up or whether further support is needed. For both universal screening and progress monitoring, it is important to select measurement tools that provide meaningful information to inform instructional decisions.

Identifying Children for the *Story Friends* Program

The first step in identifying children for the *Story Friends* program involves screening. Information from universal screening and progress monitoring assessments can be used to identify children who are good candidates for Tier 2 supplemental instruction, such as the *Story Friends* curriculum, designed to support children who exhibit delays in oral language development.

The *Story Friends* program provides a *Decision-Making Framework Teacher Questionnaire* on page 115 of this Teacher Guide as a screening tool to help you identify children who will most likely benefit from participating in the program. Note that Part I of the questionnaire (Oral Language Skills) is directly related to identifying children who may benefit from *Story Friends*. Part III (Child Characteristics) is indirectly related because it may provide indications whether the child is a better candidate for small group versus individualized instruction. To identify children to include in your small group, Tier 2 instruction versus individualized or Tier 3 instruction, you might look at the lowest-scored questionnaires to determine where to place children.

You also may choose to use other existing assessment procedures to identify children who have limited oral language skills or who are demonstrating delays in oral vocabulary and comprehension skills. Two general outcome measures that are good indicators of vocabulary and comprehension development are Individual Growth and Development Indicators (IGDIs; McConnell, Bradfield, Wackerle-Hollman, & Rodriguez, 2015), *Picture Naming* and *Which One Doesn't Belong*. For example, 4-year-old children who can label 11 of 15 pictures on the Picture Naming IGDI would seem to be developing normally (see norms and benchmarks at http://www.myigdis.com/preschool-assessments/early-literacy-assessments/). In contrast, children who perform below the benchmark for this measure might be appropriate candidates for the *Story Friends* program. However, children with very limited oral language skills (who can label two or fewer pictures on the Picture Naming IGDI) are unlikely to have sufficient oral language skills to benefit from participating in the *Story Friends* program.

Information from additional sources, including teacher questionnaires and observations, can be used in combination with universal screening measures. Teacher questionnaires that ask about specific language and learning behaviors can be effective in identifying children who are good candidates for Tier 2 supplemental instruction. For example, teachers might rate children on descriptors, such as "*This child tells simple stories that make sense*" or "*This child learns new words without difficulty.*" Educators will also want to consider information about child behavior. For example, items, such as "*This child follows directions without the need for frequent prompting*" and "*This child cooperates with peers positively*" can be informative. Those children who struggle to learn in small group settings might be better served by one-to-one instruction.

In order to benefit from the *Story Friends* program, children need adequate English language skills to understand the stories and embedded lessons. English language learners who cannot label at least two pictures on the Picture Naming IGDI would not have the English language skills necessary to benefit from the *Story Friends* curriculum.

Screening and teacher questionnaires are not high-stakes testing; they provide a means of identifying children who are likely to benefit from Tier 2 instructional support. Progress monitoring IGDIs or other assessments can be administered to clarify whether the child demonstrates delays in oral language. However, the idea is to identify children quickly so that adequate support can be provided to help them get caught up. As indicated previously in the description of the RTI approach, adjustments in instructional tiers can be made based on children's progress. *Story Friends* provides curriculum-based measures that provide timely information on child language learning and development.

REFERENCE

McConnell, S., Bradfield, T., Wackerle-Hollman, A., & Rodriguez, M. (2015). *Individual Growth and Development Indicators of Early Literacy* (2nd ed.-Universal Screening ed.). Saint Paul, MN: Early Learning Labs.

Story Friends Assessments

Two vocabulary assessments, Concept Words Pre- and Posttests and Unit Vocabulary Assessments, measure the learning outcomes of instructional goals and provide opportunities for progress monitoring. The Pacing Charts on pages 106–107 of this Teacher Guide will help you track your progress monitoring schedule.

Concept Words Pre- and Posttests

Concept Words Pre- and Posttests are administered before and after each storybook series, *Jungle Friends* and *Forest Friends*. Assessment Cards accompany the Concept Words assessments. The Concept Words Pre- and Posttests appear on pages 89–90 and 97–98 of this Teacher Guide. The following are components for *Jungle Friends* Concept Words assessments:

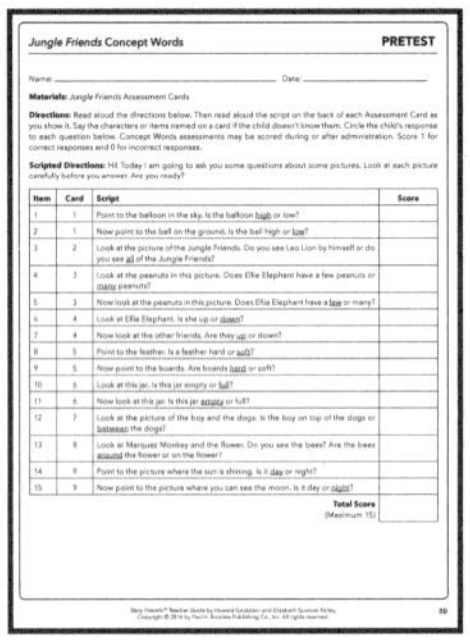
Jungle Friends Concept Words PRETEST

Jungle Friends Concept Words Pretest, p 89

Jungle Friends Concept Words POSTTEST

Jungle Friends Concept Words Posttest, p 90

Jungle Friends Concept Words Assessment Cards are used for both pre- and posttests.

Explicit instruction is provided for one or two concept words, such as *all* and *up/down*, in each storybook (except for the introductory and review books). There are four Concept Words assessments: one pretest and one posttest for each of the two storybook series. The *Jungle Friends* pre- and posttests share a set of nine Assessment Cards that correspond to the nine items on each assessment. Another set of nine Assessment Cards accompanies the storybook series *Forest Friends* Concept Words Pre-and Posttests.

Administering Concept Words Pre- and Posttests

Concept Words pre- and posttests are individually administered and take about five minutes. You will need the pre- and posttests on pages 89–90 and 97–98 of this Teacher Guide and their accompanying Assessment Cards. To introduce the tests, use the following script, which also appears on each pre- and posttest:

> Hi! Today I am going to ask you some questions about some pictures. Look at each picture carefully before you answer. Are you ready?

Show each card and read aloud the back of each card. Say the characters or items named if the child is not familiar with them. Circle the response to each item.

Scoring Concept Words Pre- and Posttests

Concept Words pre- and posttests may be scored during or after administration. Circle 0 for incorrect answers and 1 for correct answers.

Unit Vocabulary Assessments

Unit Vocabulary Assessments measure children's acquisition of program vocabulary for each unit of instruction. The six assessments are administered after each of six instructional units. Each unit represents four weeks of explicit vocabulary instruction. The Unit Vocabulary Assessments appear on pages 91–96 and 99–104 of this Teacher Guide.

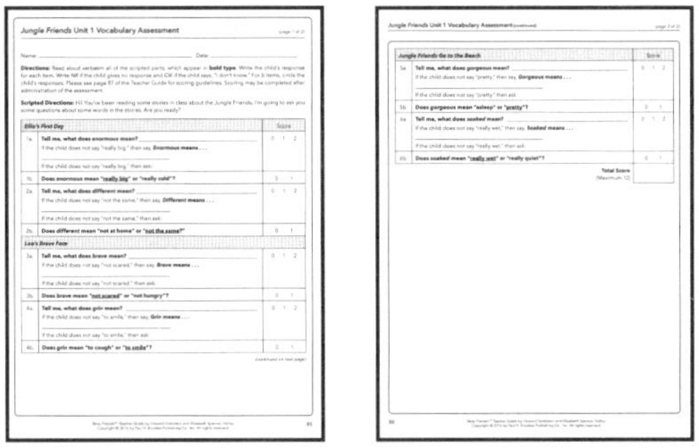

Jungle Friends Unit 1 Vocabulary Assessment, pp 91-92

Each Unit Vocabulary Assessment tests six vocabulary words from the three storybooks in each unit, providing items for two explicitly taught words per storybook. Assessment items appear as definitional or recognition vocabulary items. Definitional vocabulary items refer to open-ended questions that ask children to provide a definition of a vocabulary word. Recognition vocabulary items ask children to select the correct definition from two choices.

Definitional Vocabulary Item	**Recognition Vocabulary Item**
1a. Tell me, what does *brave* mean?	1b. Does *brave* mean "not scared" or "not hungry"?

Administering Unit Vocabulary Assessments

You will need 5–6 minutes to administer individually each Unit Vocabulary Assessment. The assessments begin on pages 91 and 99 of this Teacher Guide. To get started, use the following script, which also appears on each assessment:

> Hi! You've been reading some stories in class about the Jungle Friends. I'm going to ask you some questions about some words in the stories. Are you ready?

To ensure fidelity of the assessments, read aloud *verbatim* all of the scripted parts in the assessment, which appear in **bold type**. When you see **Tell me, what does enormous mean?** deliver the vocabulary item as it is written; do NOT paraphrase as, for example, "*We learned about the word enormous. What does that mean?*"

Administering Vocabulary Items

1. Begin with the definitional vocabulary item (e.g., 1a).
2. If the child gives a correct definition, continue to the next definitional vocabulary item (e.g., 2a). If the child doesn't respond or answers incorrectly, give a prompt: "*Enormous* means. . . ." Then if the child responds correctly, continue to the next definitional vocabulary item (e.g., 2a). If the child doesn't respond or answers incorrectly, give the recognition vocabulary item (e.g., 1b).
3. Continue to the next definitional vocabulary item (e.g., 2a).

Examples of Administering Vocabulary Items

What if . . .	Example	Action
. . . the child omits the"really" or the "to" in the definition?	A: **Tell me, what does *enormous* mean?** C: *Big.* A: **Tell me, what does *leap* mean?** C: *Jump.*	These responses are correct. Continue to the next definitional vocabulary item.
. . . the child provides a variation that includes the words in the definition?	A: **Tell me, what does *enormous* mean?** C: *Big, like an elephant.* A: **Tell me, what does *leap* mean?** C: *Jumping in the air.*	These responses are correct. Continue to the next definitional vocabulary item.
. . . you are not sure if the child's response is correct?	A: **Tell me, what does *brave* mean?** C: *Fearless.* A: **Tell me, what does *soaked* mean?** C: *All covered in water.*	Deliver the prompt or move to the recognition item.
. . . the child provides a response other than the choices for the recognition item?	A: **Does enormous mean "really big" or "really cold"?** C: *All wet.*	Write in the child's response.

A, administrator; C, child.

- The definition of each vocabulary word as taught is underscored in the *b* assessment items. Correct responses can include the exact wording of the definition, synonyms, or variations that include the vocabulary words.
- You may repeat items one time at the child's request or when it appears the child was not paying attention.
- If the child seems confused about how to respond to the prompt, include "you finish it" in the prompt. For example, "You finish it . . . *enormous* means. . . ."

Examples of Correctly Administered Items

Example A	Example B
A: **Tell me, what does *gorgeous* mean?** C: *Pretty.* A: Great thinking! (pause) **Tell me, what does *soaked* mean?** C: *I don't know.* A: ***Soaked* means . . .** (pause) C: *Take a bath.* A: **Does *soaked* mean "really wet" or "really quiet"?** C: *Really wet.* A: Nice work!	A: **Tell me, what does *gorgeous* mean?** C: *Cute.* A: (pause) ***Gorgeous* means . . .** C: (shrugs shoulders) A: **Does *gorgeous* mean "asleep" or "pretty"?** C: *Asleep.* A: Good listening. **Tell me, what does *soaked* mean?** C: *Really wet.* A: Nice work!

A, administrator; C, child.

Recording Responses on Unit Vocabulary Assessments

Record word-for-word children's responses to each item on the write-on lines provided on the assessments. If a child does not respond, record *NR* and continue to the next item. If a child says, "I don't know," record *IDK* and continue to the next item.

Scoring Unit Vocabulary Assessments

Scoring can be completed after administering the assessments by evaluating the responses you recorded. For definitional vocabulary items, score 2, 1, or 0. For recognition vocabulary items, score 1 or 0. Scoring guidelines and example responses appear in the following tables.

Scoring Guidelines for Definitional Vocabulary Items

Score	Description of Child's Response	Prompts and Sample Responses		
		Tell me, what does *soaked* mean?	**Tell me, what does *brave* mean?**	**Tell me, what does *hurry* mean?**
2	Gives definition taught in embedded lesson.	*- Really wet.* *- Wet.*	*- Not scared.* *- You not scared.*	*- To go fast.* *- Going fast.*
	Gives reasonable definition in own words.	*- A lot of water on you.* *- All wet and drippy.*	*- Not afraid of nothin'.* *- Don't be scared.*	*- Moving fast.* *- Go quick.*
	Gives synonym.	*- Drenched.*	*- Tough.*	*- Rush.*
	Uses definition in a meaningful phrase or sentence or provides a definition example.	*- Really wet, like when you stand in the rain.*	*- Not scared of nothin', even the dark.*	*- You go fast, like when you're late for school.*
1	Gives partial definition or shows partial understanding.	*- Playing in the rain.*	*- Doing scary stuff.* *- You save people.*	*- Fast.* *- To run.* *- You're running.*
	Uses target word in a phrase or sentence that provides a meaningful example or information about the word.	*- I'm soaked when I get out of the tub.* *- To soak in the water.*	*- You're brave to go and fight a monster.* *- You be brave at scary place.*	*- Hurry to get to a place.* *- I hurry up and leave the house 'cause I'm late.*
	Uses target word in a phrase or sentence that relates narrowly to the book or lesson.	*- Really wet clothes.* *- Your hair is wet and soaked.*	*- Superman not scared.* *- You not scared to fight a tiger.*	*- I need to go fast to get to my class on time.*
	Provides example of the word.	*- A wave got you wet.* *- You need towel to dry yourself.*	*- Leo's not afraid of the dentist.* *- Not afraid of school.*	*- Go fast to the circus.* *- Hurry to catch the bus.*
0	Gives incorrect response.	*- Dry.* *- Smoke.* *- Toaked.*	*- Scared of people.* *- Break.* *- Mad.*	*- Follow.* *- You go the wrong way.*
	Gives unrelated or nonsensical response.	*- I can write my name.* *- You or they're old.*	*- Pencil; do your work.* *- Don't be touchin' it.*	*- You mean.* *- He said no you leave.*
	Gives related but inadequate response.	*- In the tub.* *- Drown in water pool.*	*- Strong* *- If you go in the cave.*	*- Get somewhere.* *- You're late.*
	Repeats target word or uses word as bulk of definition; shows no knowledge of meaning.	*- You soaked.* *- All soaked up.* *- Soaked and cold.* *- Getting clothes soaked.*	*- That you're brave.* *- Brave.* *- People being brave.* *- You brave when it's cold.*	*- Hurry up.* *- You got to hurry.* *- Hurry, hurry, hurry!* *- Hurry in the car.*

Scoring Guidelines for Recognition Vocabulary Items

Score	Description of Child's Response	Prompts and Sample Responses		
		Does *soaked* mean "really big" or "really wet"?	**Does *brave* mean "not scared" or "not tired"?**	**Does *hurry* mean "to go fast" or "to kick hard"?**
1	Correct response.	- *Really wet.*	- *Not scared.*	- *To go fast.*
0	No response or incorrect response.	- No response or *I don't know.* - *Really cold.* - *Hot.*	- No response or *I don't know.* - *Not tired.* - *Reckless.*	- No response or *I don't know.* - *To kick hard.* - *Excited.*

Progress Monitoring in *Story Friends*

The RTI approach uses progress monitoring to ensure that each child receives the level of support and instruction to ensure progress or staying on-level. The curriculum-based measures of *Story Friends*, as well as teacher observations, will help inform your decisions about children's instructional paths.

The high-frequency concept words taught in *Story Friends* may be known by many preschoolers, so the Concept Words Pre- and Posttest scores may not differ markedly. However, reviewing these essential words in an academic setting will help prepare children for later grades.

The *Story Friends* Unit Vocabulary Assessments measure children's acquisition of explicitly taught vocabulary and provide information on the effects of Tier 2 instruction. Typically, children will demonstrate mastery on one third to one half of the targeted vocabulary words. In some cases, a child may improve in performance after several weeks in the program. If a child demonstrates mastery on most of the assessed words, then the intervention may no longer be needed. Further confirmation, such as word knowledge when a Unit Vocabulary Assessment is used as a pretest, will help inform whether continued intervention is necessary.

Teacher observations at the Listening Center can also be used as a source of information: if a child responds appropriately to comprehension questions and vocabulary lessons during the first listen to a story, the child may not require the repeated readings included in the *Story Friends* program. In addition, another progress monitoring measure, such as the Picture Naming IGDI, might confirm that the child will most likely progress well in the general classroom curriculum.

Alternatively, information from the Unit Vocabulary Assessments and teacher observations may indicate that a child is not responding well to the *Story Friends* intervention. If a child does not demonstrate mastery on at least two words on a Unit Vocabulary Assessment, or if teacher observations of responses to comprehension questions and vocabulary lessons at the Listening Center indicate that the child is not responding well to the Tier 2 instruction, you might consider providing another tier of support as individualized Tier 3 instruction. Using the *Story Friends* materials, a teacher or aide might pause the recording after comprehension questions or during vocabulary lessons to allow more response time. A child might also benefit from individual sessions that include prompts and feedback contingent on correct responses.

Information from two consecutive units of instruction, including teacher observations and Vocabulary Assessments, will help you make decisions about children's continued participation in the intervention.

Progress Monitoring Guidelines

On Two Consecutive Vocabulary Assessments . . .	
If a child scores:	**You might consider:**
12	Tier 1 instruction
5–11	Continuing Tier 2 program
0–4	Tier 3 intervention

Jungle Friends Concept Words **PRETEST**

Name: ______________________ Date: ______________

Materials: *Jungle Friends* Assessment Cards

Directions: Read aloud the directions below. Then read aloud the script on the back of each Assessment Card as you show it. Say the characters or items named on a card if the child doesn't know them. Circle the child's response to each question below. Concept Words assessments may be scored during or after administration. Score 1 for correct responses and 0 for incorrect responses.

Scripted Directions: Hi! Today I am going to ask you some questions about some pictures. Look at each picture carefully before you answer. Are you ready?

Item	Card	Script	Score
1	1	Point to the balloon in the sky. Is the balloon high or low?	
2	1	Now point to the ball on the ground. Is the ball high or low?	
3	2	Look at the picture of the Jungle Friends. Do you see Leo Lion by himself or do you see all of the Jungle Friends?	
4	3	Look at the peanuts in this picture. Does Ellie Elephant have a few peanuts or many peanuts?	
5	3	Now look at the peanuts in this picture. Does Ellie Elephant have a few or many?	
6	4	Look at Ellie Elephant. Is she up or down?	
7	4	Now look at the other friends. Are they up or down?	
8	5	Point to the feather. Is a feather hard or soft?	
9	5	Now point to the boards. Are boards hard or soft?	
10	6	Look at this jar. Is this jar empty or full?	
11	6	Now look at this jar. Is this jar empty or full?	
12	7	Look at the picture of the boy and the dogs. Is the boy on top of the dogs or between the dogs?	
13	8	Look at Marquez Monkey and the flower. Do you see the bees? Are the bees around the flower or on the flower?	
14	9	Point to the picture where the sun is shining. Is it day or night?	
15	9	Now point to the picture where you can see the moon. Is it day or night?	
		Total Score (Maximum 15)	

Jungle Friends Concept Words **POSTTEST**

Name: ______________________ Date: ______________

Materials: *Jungle Friends* Assessment Cards

Directions: Read aloud the directions below. Then read aloud the script on the back of each Assessment Card as you show it. Say the characters or items named on a card if the child doesn't know them. Circle the child's response to each question below. Concept Words assessments may be scored during or after administration. Score 1 for correct responses and 0 for incorrect responses.

Scripted Directions: Hi! Today I am going to ask you some questions about some pictures. Look at each picture carefully before you answer. Are you ready?

Item	Card	Script	Score
1	7	Look at the picture of the boy and the dogs. Is the boy on top of the dogs or between the dogs?	
2	4	Look at Ellie Elephant. Is she up or down?	
3	4	Now look at the other friends. Are they up or down?	
4	1	Point to the balloon in the sky. Is the balloon high or low?	
5	1	Now point to the ball on the ground. Is the ball high or low?	
6	2	Look at the picture of the Jungle Friends. Do you see Leo Lion by himself or do you see all of the Jungle Friends?	
7	5	Point to the feather. Is a feather hard or soft?	
8	5	Now point to the boards. Are boards hard or soft?	
9	3	Look at the peanuts in this picture. Does Ellie Elephant have a few peanuts or many peanuts?	
10	3	Now look at the peanuts in this picture. Does Ellie Elephant have a few or many?	
11	9	Point to the picture where the sun is shining. Is it day or night?	
12	9	Now point to the picture where you can see the moon. Is it day or night?	
13	6	Look at this jar. Is this jar empty or full?	
14	6	Now look at this jar. Is this jar empty or full?	
15	8	Look at Marquez Monkey and the flower. Do you see the bees? Are the bees around the flower or on the flower?	
		Total Score (Maximum 15)	

Jungle Friends Unit 1 Vocabulary Assessment

Name: ______________________ Date: ______________

Directions: Read aloud *verbatim* all of the scripted parts, which appear in **bold type**. Write the child's response for each item. Write *NR* if the child gives no response and *IDK* if the child says, "I don't know." For *b* items, circle the child's responses. Please see page 87 of the Teacher Guide for scoring guidelines. Scoring may be completed after administration of the assessment.

Scripted Directions: Hi! You've been reading some stories in class about the Jungle Friends. I'm going to ask you some questions about some words in the stories. Are you ready?

Ellie's First Day		Score
1a.	**Tell me, what does *enormous* mean?** ______________ If the child does not say "really big," then say, ***Enormous* means . . .** ______________ If the child does not say "really big," then ask:	0 1 2
1b.	**Does *enormous* mean "<u>really big</u>" or "really cold"?**	0 1
2a.	**Tell me, what does *different* mean?** ______________ If the child does not say "not the same," then say, ***Different* means . . .** ______________ If the child does not say "not the same," then ask:	0 1 2
2b.	**Does *different* mean "not at home" or "<u>not the same</u>?"**	0 1
Leo's Brave Face		
3a.	**Tell me, what does *brave* mean?** ______________ If the child does not say "not scared," then say, ***Brave* means . . .** ______________ If the child does not say "not scared," then ask:	0 1 2
3b.	**Does *brave* mean "<u>not scared</u>" or "not hungry"?**	0 1
4a.	**Tell me, what does *grin* mean?** ______________ If the child does not say "to smile," then say, ***Grin* means . . .** ______________ If the child does not say "to smile," then ask:	0 1 2
4b.	**Does *grin* mean "to cough" or "<u>to smile</u>"?**	0 1

(continued on next page)

Jungle Friends Go to the Beach		Score
5a.	**Tell me, what does *gorgeous* mean?** ______________ If the child does not say "pretty," then say, ***Gorgeous* means . . .** ______________ If the child does not say "pretty," then ask:	0 1 2
5b.	**Does *gorgeous* mean "asleep" or "pretty"?**	0 1
6a.	**Tell me, what does *soaked* mean?** ______________ If the child does not say "really wet," then say, ***Soaked* means . . .** ______________ If the child does not say "really wet," then ask:	0 1 2
6b.	**Does *soaked* mean "really wet" or "really quiet"?**	0 1
	Total Score (Maximum 12)	

Jungle Friends Unit 2 Vocabulary Assessment

Name: ______________________ Date: ______________

Directions: Read aloud *verbatim* all of the scripted parts, which appear in **bold type**. Write in the child's response for each item. Write *NR* if the child gives no response and *IDK* if the child says, "I don't know." For *b* items, circle the child's responses. Please see page 87 of the Teacher Guide for scoring guidelines. Scoring may be completed after administration of the assessment.

Scripted Directions: Hi! You've been reading some stories in class about the Jungle Friends. I'm going to ask you some questions about some words in the stories. Are you ready?

Marquez Monkeys Around		Score
1a.	**Tell me, what does *reckless* mean?** ______________ If the child does not say "not safe," then say, ***Reckless* means . . .** ______________ If the child does not say "not safe," then ask:	0 1 2
1b.	**Does *reckless* mean "not tired" or "<u>not safe</u>?"**	0 1
2a.	**Tell me, what does *ruin* mean?** ______________ If the child does not say "to mess up," then say, ***Ruin* means . . .** ______________ If the child does not say "to mess up," then ask:	0 1 2
2b.	**Does *ruin* mean "<u>to mess up</u>" or "to move over"?**	0 1
If Elephants Could Fly		
3a.	**Tell me, what does *imagine* mean?** ______________ If the child does not say "to pretend," then say, ***Imagine* means . . .** ______________ If the child does not say "to pretend," then ask:	0 1 2
3b.	**Does *imagine* mean "to open" or "<u>to pretend</u>"?**	0 1
4a.	**Tell me, what does *soar* mean?** ______________ If the child does not say "to fly," then say, ***Soar* means . . .** ______________ If the child does not say "to fly," then ask:	0 1 2
4b.	**Does soar mean "<u>to fly</u>" or "to choose"?**	0 1

(continued on next page)

Leo Loses His Roar		Score
5a.	**Tell me, what does *ill* mean?** ______________ If the child does not say "sick," then say, ***Ill* means . . .** ______________ If the child does not say "sick," then ask:	0 1 2
5b.	**Does *ill* mean "shiny" or "<u>sick</u>"?**	0 1
6a.	**Tell me, what does *comfort* mean?** ______________ If the child does not say "to make you feel better," then say, ***Comfort* means . . .** ______________ If the child does not say "to make you feel better," then ask:	0 1 2
6b.	**Does *comfort* mean "<u>to make you feel better</u>" or "to put your toys away"?**	0 1
	Total Score (Maximum 12)	

Jungle Friends Unit 3 Vocabulary Assessment

Name: ______________________ Date: ______________________

Directions: Read aloud *verbatim* all of the scripted parts, which appear in **bold type**. Write in the child's response for each item. Write *NR* if the child gives no response and *IDK* if the child says, "I don't know." For *b* items, circle the child's responses. Please see page 87 of the Teacher Guide for scoring guidelines. Scoring may be completed after administration of the assessment.

Scripted Directions: Hi! You've been reading some stories in class about the Jungle Friends. I'm going to ask you some questions about some words in the stories. Are you ready?

Ellie Gets Stuck		Score
1a.	**Tell me, what does *leap* mean?** ______________________ If the child does not say "to jump," then say, ***Leap* means . . .** ______________________ If the child does not say "to jump," then ask:	0 1 2
1b.	**Does *leap* mean "to crawl" or "<u>to jump</u>"?**	0 1
2a.	**Tell me, what does *pause* mean?** ______________________ If the child does not say "to stop," then say, ***Pause* means . . .** ______________________ If the child does not say "to stop," then ask:	0 1 2
2b.	**Does *pause* mean "<u>to stop</u>" or "to climb"?**	0 1
A New Jungle Friend		
3a.	**Tell me, what does *speedy* mean?** ______________________ If the child does not say "fast," then say, ***Speedy* means . . .** ______________________ If the child does not say "fast," then ask:	0 1 2
3b.	**Does *speedy* mean "round" or "<u>fast</u>"?**	0 1
4a.	**Tell me, what does *wise* mean?** ______________________ If the child does not say "smart," then say, ***Wise* means . . .** ______________________ If the child does not say "smart," then ask:	0 1 2
4b.	**Does *wise* mean "<u>smart</u>" or "clean"?**	0 1

(continued on next page)

Marquez's Backwards Day		Score
5a.	**Tell me, what does *ridiculous* mean?** ______________________ If the child does not say "silly," then say, ***Ridiculous* means . . .** ______________________ If the child does not say "silly," then ask:	0 1 2
5b.	**Does *ridiculous* mean "silly" or "tall"?**	0 1
6a.	**Tell me, what does *tumble* mean?** ______________________ If the child does not say "to fall," then say, ***Tumble* means . . .** ______________________ If the child does not say "to fall," then ask:	0 1 2
6b.	**Does *tumble* mean "to sing" or "to fall"?**	0 1
	Total Score (Maximum 12)	

Forest Friends Concept Words **PRETEST**

Name: ______________________ Date: ______________

Materials: *Forest Friends* Assessment Cards

Directions: Read aloud the directions below. Then read aloud the script on the back of each Assessment Card as you show it. Say the characters or items named on a card if the child doesn't know them. Circle the child's response to each question below. Concept Words assessments may be scored during or after administration. Score 1 for correct responses and 0 for incorrect responses.

Scripted Directions: Hi! Today I am going to ask you some questions about some pictures. Look at each picture carefully before you answer. Are you ready?

Item	Card	Script	Score
1	1	Point to the cat. Is the cat the largest or the smallest?	
2	1	Now point to the bee. Is the bee the largest or the smallest?	
3	2	Look at the Forest Friends walking in a line to Suki's tree. Point to Bobby Bear. Is Bobby first or last?	
4	2	Now point to Pablo Porcupine. Is Pablo first or last?	
5	3	Point to Bobby Bear. Is Bobby Bear short or tall?	
6	3	Now point to Suki Squirrel. Is Suki Squirrel short or tall?	
7	4	Can you find Grandmother's den in this picture? Are the friends near or far from the den?	
8	4	Now find Grandmother's den. Are the friends near or far from the den?	
9	5	Point to Suki Squirrel. Is Suki at the top of the hill or at the bottom of the hill?	
10	5	Now point to Bobby Bear. Is Bobby at the top of the hill or at the bottom of the hill?	
11	6	Point to the picture where there is snow on the ground. Is it winter or spring?	
12	6	Now point to the picture where there are leaves on the trees. Is it winter or spring?	
13	7	Look at Pablo Porcupine talking. Is Pablo being loud or quiet?	
14	7	Now look at Pablo Porcupine shouting. Is Pablo being loud or quiet?	
15	8	Point to the girl. Is she in the cart or out of the cart?	
16	8	Now point to the boy. Is he in the cart or out of the cart?	
17	9	Point to the pink shoes. Are the pink shoes new or old?	
18	9	Now point to the other shoes. Are they new or old?	
		Total Score (Maximum 18)	

Forest Friends Concept Words **POSTTEST**

Name: ______________________________ Date: ____________________

Materials: *Forest Friends* Assessment Cards

Directions: Read aloud the directions below. Then read aloud the script on the back of each Assessment Card as you show it. Say the characters or items named on a card if the child doesn't know them. Circle the child's response to each question below. Concept Words assessments may be scored during or after administration. Score 1 for correct responses and 0 for incorrect responses.

Scripted Directions: Hi! Today I am going to ask you some questions about some pictures. Look at each picture carefully before you answer. Are you ready?

Item	Card	Script	Score
1	6	Point to the picture where there is snow on the ground. Is it winter or spring?	
2	6	Now point to the picture where there are leaves on the trees. Is it winter or spring?	
3	5	Point to Suki Squirrel. Is Suki at the top of the hill or at the bottom of the hill?	
4	5	Now point to Bobby Bear. Is Bobby at the top of the hill or at the bottom of the hill?	
5	1	Point to the cat. Is the cat the largest or the smallest?	
6	1	Now point to the bee. Is the bee the largest or the smallest?	
7	7	Look at Pablo Porcupine talking. Is Pablo being loud or quiet?	
8	7	Now look at Pablo Porcupine shouting. Is Pablo being loud or quiet?	
9	2	Look at the Forest Friends walking in a line to Suki's tree. Point to Bobby Bear. Is Bobby first or last?	
10	2	Now point to Pablo Porcupine. Is Pablo first or last?	
11	9	Point to the pink shoes. Are the pink shoes new or old?	
12	9	Now point to the other shoes. Are they new or old?	
13	4	Can you find Grandmother's den in this picture? Are the friends near or far from the den?	
14	4	Now find Grandmother's den. Are the friends near or far from the den?	
15	8	Point to the girl. Is she in the cart or out of the cart?	
16	8	Now point to the boy. Is he in the cart or out of the cart?	
17	3	Point to Bobby Bear. Is Bobby Bear short or tall?	
18	3	Now point to Suki Squirrel. Is Suki Squirrel short or tall?	
		Total Score (Maximum 18)	

Forest Friends Unit 4 Vocabulary Assessment

Name: ______________________ Date: ______________

Directions: Read aloud *verbatim* all of the scripted parts, which appear in **bold type**. Write in the child's response for each item. Write *NR* if the child gives no response and *IDK* if the child says, "I don't know." For *b* items, circle the child's responses. Please see page 87 of the Teacher Guide for scoring guidelines. Scoring may be completed after administration of the assessment.

Scripted Directions: Hi! You've been reading some stories in class about the Forest Friends. I'm going to ask you some questions about some words in the stories. Are you ready?

Pablo's Prickly Problem		Score
1a.	**Tell me, what does *terrified* mean?** ______________ If the child does not say "really scared," then say, ***Terrified* means . . .** ______________ If the child does not say "really scared," then ask:	0 1 2
1b.	**Does *terrified* mean "<u>really scared</u>" or "really bright"?**	0 1
2a.	**Tell me, what does *protect* mean?** ______________ If the child does not say "to keep someone safe," then say, ***Protect* means . . .** ______________ If the child does not say "to keep someone safe," then ask:	0 1 2
2b.	**Does *protect* mean "to talk a lot" or "<u>to keep someone safe</u>"?**	0 1
Suki's Sleepover Surprise		
3a.	**Tell me, what does *agree* mean?** ______________ If the child does not say "to say yes," then say, ***Agree* means . . .** ______________ If the child does not say "to say yes," then ask:	0 1 2
3b.	**Does *agree* mean "to walk away" or "<u>to say yes</u>"?**	0 1
4a.	**Tell me, what does *disappointed* mean?** ______________ If the child does not say "sad," then say, ***Disappointed* means . . .** ______________ If the child does not say "sad," then ask:	0 1 2
4b.	**Does *disappointed* mean "<u>sad</u>" or "dry"?**	0 1

(continued on next page)

	Bobby's EmBEARassing Visit	Score
5a.	**Tell me, what does *kind* mean?** ________________ If the child does not say "nice," then say, ***Kind* means . . .** ________________ If the child does not say "nice," then ask:	0 1 2
5b.	**Does *kind* mean "<u>nice</u>" or "slippery"?**	0 1
6a.	**Tell me, what does *accident* mean?** ________________ If the child does not say "something you didn't mean to do," then say, ***Accident* means . . .** ________________ If the child does not say "something you didn't mean to do," then ask:	0 1 2
6b.	**Does *accident* mean "something you have to do" or "<u>something you didn't mean to do</u>"?**	0 1
	Total Score (Maximum 12)	

Forest Friends Unit 5 Vocabulary Assessment

Name: ______________________________ Date: ____________________

Directions: Read aloud *verbatim* all of the scripted parts, which appear in **bold type**. Write in the child's response for each item. Write *NR* if the child gives no response and *IDK* if the child says, "I don't know." For *b* items, circle the child's responses. Please see page 87 of the Teacher Guide for scoring guidelines. Scoring may be completed after administration of the assessment.

Scripted Directions: Hi! You've been reading some stories in class about the Forest Friends. I'm going to ask you some questions about some words in the stories. Are you ready?

Fae's Nose Knows		Score
1a.	**Tell me, what does *lost* mean?** ____________ If the child does not say "you don't know where you are," then say, ***Lost* means . . .** ____________ If the child does not say "you don't know where you are," then ask:	0 1 2
1b.	**Does *lost* mean "you don't want to get up" or "you don't know where you are"?**	0 1
2a.	**Tell me, what does *worried* mean?** ____________ If the child does not say "scared something bad might happen," then say, ***Worried* means . . .** ____________ If the child does not say "scared something bad might happen," then ask:	0 1 2
2b.	**Does *worried* mean "scared something bad might happen" or "happy to go somewhere"?**	0 1
Snow Day for Fae		
3a.	**Tell me, what does *complete* mean?** ____________ If the child does not say "all done," then say, ***Complete* means . . .** ____________ If the child does not say "all done," then ask:	0 1 2
3b.	**Does *complete* mean "turned around" or "all done"?**	0 1
4a.	**Tell me, what does *frosty* mean?** ____________ If the child does not say "cold," then say, ***Frosty* means . . .** ____________ If the child does not say "cold," then ask:	0 1 2
4b.	**Does *frosty* mean "cold" or "long"?**	0 1

(continued on next page)

Where Is Bobby Bear?		Score
5a.	**Tell me, what does *exhausted* mean?** ____________________ If the child does not say "really tired," then say, ***Exhausted* means . . .** ____________________ If the child does not say "really tired," then ask:	0 1 2
5b.	**Does *exhausted* mean "really fun" or "really tired"?**	0 1
6a.	**Tell me, what does *search* mean?** ____________________ If the child does not say "to look for something," then say, ***Search* means . . .** ____________________ If the child does not say "to look for something," then ask:	0 1 2
6b.	**Does *search* mean "to yell at someone" or "to look for something"?**	0 1
	Total Score (Maximum 12)	

Forest Friends Unit 6 Vocabulary Assessment

Name: ______________________________ Date: ______________________

Directions: Read aloud *verbatim* all of the scripted parts, which appear in **bold type**. Write in the child's response for each item. Write *NR* if the child gives no response and *IDK* if the child says, "I don't know." For *b* items, circle the child's responses. Please see page 87 of the Teacher Guide for scoring guidelines. Scoring may be completed after administration of the assessment.

Scripted Directions: Hi! You've been reading some stories in class about the Forest Friends. I'm going to ask you some questions about some words in the stories. Are you ready?

Pablo's Map Matters		Score
1a.	**Tell me, what does *thrilled* mean?** ______________ If the child does not say "excited," then say, ***Thrilled* means . . .** ______________ If the child does not say "excited," then ask:	0 1 2
1b.	**Does *thrilled* mean "sorry" or "<u>excited</u>"?**	0 1
2a.	**Tell me, what does *ignore* mean?** ______________ If the child does not say "to not listen," then say, ***Ignore* means . . .** ______________ If the child does not say "to not listen," then ask:	0 1 2
2b.	**Does *ignore* mean "<u>to not listen</u>" or "to not touch?"**	0 1 2
Fae's Smelly Situation		
3a.	**Tell me, what does *horrible* mean?** ______________ If the child does not say "really bad," then say, ***Horrible* means . . .** ______________ If the child does not say "really bad," then ask:	0 1 2
3b.	**Does *horrible* mean "<u>really bad</u>" or "really soft"?**	0 1
4a.	**Tell me, what does *fail* mean?** ______________ If the child does not say "to not work," then say, ***Fail* means . . .** ______________ If the child does not say "to not work," then ask:	0 1 2
4b.	**Does *fail* mean "<u>to not work</u>" or "to not care"?**	0 1

(continued on next page)

Suki's Selfish Saturday		Score
5a.	**Tell me, what does *selfish* mean?** ________________ If the child does not say "you don't want to share," then say, ***Selfish* means . . .** ________________ If the child does not say "you don't want to share," then ask:	0 1 2
5b.	**Does *selfish* mean "you don't need help" or "<u>you don't want to share</u>"?**	0 1
6a.	**Tell me, what does *enjoy* mean?** ________________ If the child does not say "to have fun," then say, ***Enjoy* means . . .** ________________ If the child does not say "to have fun," then ask:	0 1 2
6b.	**Does *enjoy* mean "<u>to have fun</u>" or "to buy something"?**	0 1
	Total Score (Maximum 12)	

Resource Masters

The Resource Masters may be photocopied for use in your classroom; they are also available on the USB program component as fillable forms.

Story Friends: Jungle Friends Pacing Chart

Use this resource to help you plan your instructional pacing of the *Jungle Friends* series. Enter the dates you complete each component or Listen.

Unit	Week	Book/ Assessment	Day 1	Date	Day 2	Date	Day 3	Date	Day 4	Date	Day 5	Date
***Jungle Friends* Concept Words Pretest**												
1	1	*Meet the Jungle Friends*	Listen 1		Listen 2		Listen 3		Make-up day		Make-up day	
	2	*Ellie's First Day*	Listen 1		Listen 2		Listen 3		Make-up day		Make-up day	
	3	*Leo's Brave Face*	Listen 1		Listen 2		Listen 3		Make-up day		Make-up day	
	4	*Jungle Friends Go to the Beach*	Listen 1		Listen 2		Listen 3		Make-up day		Make-up day	
	5	*Jungle Friends Bake a Cake:* Review	Listen 1		Listen 2		Listen 3		Make-up day		Make-up day	
Unit 1 Vocabulary Assessment												
2	6	*Marquez Monkeys Around*	Listen 1		Listen 2		Listen 3		Make-up day		Make-up day	
	7	*If Elephants Could Fly*	Listen 1		Listen 2		Listen 3		Make-up day		Make-up day	
	8	*Leo Loses His Roar*	Listen 1		Listen 2		Listen 3		Make-up day		Make-up day	
	9	*Jungle Friends Go to the Park:* Review	Listen 1		Listen 2		Listen 3		Make-up day		Make-up day	
Unit 2 Vocabulary Assessment												
3	10	*Ellie Gets Stuck*	Listen 1		Listen 2		Listen 3		Make-up day		Make-up day	
	11	*A New Jungle Friend*	Listen 1		Listen 2		Listen 3		Make-up day		Make-up day	
	12	*Marquez's Backwards Day*	Listen 1		Listen 2		Listen 3		Make-up day		Make-up day	
	13	*Jungle Friends Swing Through the Vines:* Review	Listen 1		Listen 2		Listen 3		Make-up day		Make-up day	
Unit 3 Vocabulary Assessment												
***Jungle Friends* Concept Words Posttest**												

Story Friends: Forest Friends Pacing Chart

Use this resource to help you plan your instructional pacing of the *Forest Friends* series. Enter the dates you complete each component or listen.

Unit	Week	Book/ Assessment	Day 1	Date	Day 2	Date	Day 3	Date	Day 4	Date	Day 5	Date
***Forest Friends* Concept Words Pretest**												
4	14	*Meet the Forest Friends*	Listen 1		Listen 2		Listen 3		Make-up day		Make-up day	
	15	*Pablo's Prickly Problem*	Listen 1		Listen 2		Listen 3		Make-up day		Make-up day	
	16	*Suki's Sleepover Surprise*	Listen 1		Listen 2		Listen 3		Make-up day		Make-up day	
	17	*Bobby's EmBEARassing Visit*	Listen 1		Listen 2		Listen 3		Make-up day		Make-up day	
	18	*Suki Squirrel Goes Swimming:* Review	Listen 1		Listen 2		Listen 3		Make-up day		Make-up day	
Unit 4 Vocabulary Assessment												
5	19	*Fae's Nose Knows*	Listen 1		Listen 2		Listen 3		Make-up day		Make-up day	
	20	*Snow Day for Fae*	Listen 1		Listen 2		Listen 3		Make-up day		Make-up day	
	21	*Where Is Bobby Bear?*	Listen 1		Listen 2		Listen 3		Make-up day		Make-up day	
	22	*Pablo Packs a Picnic:* Review	Listen 1		Listen 2		Listen 3		Make-up day		Make-up day	
Unit 5 Vocabulary Assessment												
6	23	*Pablo's Map Matters*	Listen 1		Listen 2		Listen 3		Make-up day		Make-up day	
	24	*Fae's Smelly Situation*	Listen 1		Listen 2		Listen 3		Make-up day		Make-up day	
	25	*Suki's Selfish Saturday*	Listen 1		Listen 2		Listen 3		Make-up day		Make-up day	
	26	*Forest Friends Go to the Library:* Review	Listen 1		Listen 2		Listen 3		Make-up day		Make-up day	
Unit 6 Vocabulary Assessment												
***Forest Friends* Concept Words Posttest**												

Jungle Friends Unit 1 Attendance Log

Directions: Record the date each time children listen to a story.

Unit 1	Week 1 *Meet the Jungle Friends*			Week 2 *Ellie's First Day*			Week 3 *Leo's Brave Face*			Week 4 *Jungle Friends Go to the Beach*			Week 5 *Jungle Friends Bake a Cake: Review*		
Child	**Listen 1**	**Listen 2**	**Listen 3**	**Listen 1**	**Listen 2**	**Listen 3**	**Listen 1**	**Listen 2**	**Listen 3**	**Listen 1**	**Listen 2**	**Listen 3**	**Listen 1**	**Listen 2**	**Listen 3**

Jungle Friends Unit 2 Attendance Log

Directions: Record the date each time children listen to a story.

Unit 2	Week 6 *Marquez Monkeys Around*			Week 7 *If Elephants Could Fly*			Week 8 *Leo Loses His Roar*			Week 9 *Jungle Friends Go to the Park:* Review		
Child	**Listen 1**	**Listen 2**	**Listen 3**	**Listen 1**	**Listen 2**	**Listen 3**	**Listen 1**	**Listen 2**	**Listen 3**	**Listen 1**	**Listen 2**	**Listen 3**

Jungle Friends Unit 3 Attendance Log

Directions: Record the date each time children listen to a story.

Unit 3	Week 10 *Ellie Gets Stuck*			Week 11 *A New Jungle Friend*			Week 12 *Marquez's Backwards Day*			Week 13 *Jungle Friends Swing Through the Vines: Review*		
Child	**Listen 1**	**Listen 2**	**Listen 3**	**Listen 1**	**Listen 2**	**Listen 3**	**Listen 1**	**Listen 2**	**Listen 3**	**Listen 1**	**Listen 2**	**Listen 3**

Forest Friends Unit 4 Attendance Log

Directions: Record the date each time children listen to a story.

Unit 4	Week 14 *Meet the Forest Friends*			Week 15 *Pablo's Prickly Problem*			Week 16 *Suki's Sleepover Surprise*			Week 17 *Bobby's EmBEARassing Visit*			Week 18 *Suki Squirrel Goes Swimming:* Review		
Child	**Listen 1**	**Listen 2**	**Listen 3**	**Listen 1**	**Listen 2**	**Listen 3**	**Listen 1**	**Listen 2**	**Listen 3**	**Listen 1**	**Listen 2**	**Listen 3**	**Listen 1**	**Listen 2**	**Listen 3**

Forest Friends Unit 5 Attendance Log

Directions: Record the date each time children listen to a story.

Unit 5	Week 19 *Fae's Nose Knows*			Week 20 *Snow Day for Fae*			Week 21 *Where Is Bobby Bear?*			Week 22 *Pablo Packs a Picnic: Review*		
Child	**Listen 1**	**Listen 2**	**Listen 3**	**Listen 1**	**Listen 2**	**Listen 3**	**Listen 1**	**Listen 2**	**Listen 3**	**Listen 1**	**Listen 2**	**Listen 3**

Forest Friends Unit 6 Attendance Log

Directions: Record the date each time children listen to a story.

Unit 6	Week 23 *Pablo's Map Matters*			Week 24 *Fae's Smelly Situation*			Week 25 *Suki's Selfish Saturday*			Week 26 *Forest Friends Go to the Library:* Review		
Child	**Listen 1**	**Listen 2**	**Listen 3**	**Listen 1**	**Listen 2**	**Listen 3**	**Listen 1**	**Listen 2**	**Listen 3**	**Listen 1**	**Listen 2**	**Listen 3**

Listening Center

Quick Reference Guide

Before each Listening Center session:

- ☑ Children are in their assigned seats.
- ☑ Each child has the correct storybook.
- ☑ Each child has headphones on and is ready to begin listening.
- ☑ Children have enough space to turn pages.
- ☑ I am close enough to help children turn pages.

During each Listening Center session:

- ☑ The correct audio is playing.
- ☑ Children are on the correct page.
- ☑ Children are responding to questions.
- ☑ Children are engaged and participating.

After each Listening Center session:

- ☑ I completed the Attendance Log.

At the end of each 5-day period:

- ☑ Each child listened to the storybook three times.
- ☑ The next storybooks are ready and the audio is cued up.
- ☑ The audio equipment is functioning properly.

Decision-Making Framework Teacher Questionnaire

Directions: For each question, make a check mark in the box that best indicates how often each child displays each skill or behavior. Please check **only ONE box** for each question.

Child's Name:	**Never**	**Rarely**	**Often**	**Always**
PART I: ORAL LANGUAGE SKILLS				
Expressive Language Skills (Spoken Language)				
1. This child uses simple grammatically correct sentences (e.g., does not exhibit pronoun confusion, tense verb errors, word order reversals).				
2. This child produces sentences containing a variety of words including nouns, verbs, and adjectives.				
3. This child tells short, understandable narratives about personal events.				
Vocabulary Skills				
4. This child identifies and labels most common objects in the classroom.				
5. This child correctly selects a toy or classroom object when described using color, location, or other descriptors.				
6. This child categorizes vocabulary, and names words belonging to categories (e.g., vehicles, animals, toys).				
PART II: COMPREHENSION SKILLS				
7. This child follows two- and three-step directions.				
8. This child answers explicit *who, what, where, when,* and *how* questions.				
9. This child understands implicit questions requiring inferencing or predicting what is happening in the story.				
10. This child retells simple stories.				
PART III: CHILD CHARACTERISTICS				
11. This child follows directions without the need for frequent prompting (e.g., hands to yourself).				
12. This child requires multiple teaching strategies to learn something new (e.g., modeling, extra prompting, repeated practice, rephrasing, manipulatives).				
13. This child needs high levels of positive verbal reinforcement to complete a task.				
14. This child transitions between preferred and nonpreferred activities without difficulty.				
15. This child cooperates with peers (e.g., shares, takes turns, waits for turn).				
16. This child initiates social interactions with peers adequately.				

From Bradfield, T.A., & McConnell, S.R. (2012). Teacher questionnaire of language and comprehension skills among preschool children. Technical Report, Center on Response to Intervention in Early Childhood, University of Minnesota, Minneapolis, MN. Adapted by permission.

The Research Behind *Story Friends*

Howard Goldstein
Elizabeth Spencer Kelley

MILLIE™
MULTITIERED INTERVENTIONS FOR LANGUAGE & LITERACY IN EARLY CHILDHOOD

Overview

Story Friends is a supplemental curriculum for teaching preschoolers and some kindergartners challenging academic vocabulary, basic concept words, and how to answer questions about stories. Although the curriculum may have widespread appeal to all preschoolers, these stories with embedded lessons were designed to promote language development among children who are at risk for later reading problems because of their weak language skills. Thus, our research focused on effects of the curriculum with at-risk prekindergarten (pre-K) populations. Because the stories and lessons are delivered using audio recordings, *Story Friends* can easily be implemented to small groups of children by teacher assistants or other paraprofessionals. Teachers or other professional staff members are provided tools to help with the selection of students and the monitoring of instruction and children's progress, and *Story Friends* contains a framework for deciding who should be receiving instruction with and without other modifications. Two book series totaling 26 books offer children interactive instruction for one book per week, 10–15 minutes per day. This is sufficient to provide children with many opportunities to learn vocabulary and comprehension skills that will help prepare them for later academic success.

Program Foundation

Children enter early childhood programs with diverse early language and literacy experiences. A substantial number of children, especially many children growing up in low-income homes, have limited oral language skills that place them at risk for later reading disabilities. For example, Qi, Kaiser, Milan, and Hancock (2006) reported that preschoolers enrolled in Head Start scored an average of approximately 1.5 standard deviations below the normative mean on a standardized measure of receptive vocabulary, the Peabody Picture Vocabulary Test–Third Edition (PPVT-III; Dunn & Dunn, 1997). Preschool children with limited oral language skills, including vocabulary, are at risk for reading disabilities in later school years (National Early Literacy Panel, 2008). Students who fall behind their peers in language and literacy development often continue to struggle throughout the school years (Foster & Miller, 2007; National Center for Education Statistics, 2014). Thus, there is a need for curricula that enhance the language skills of children who demonstrate weaknesses in language development.

Response to intervention (RTI) offers a framework for preventing language and reading disorders. Often called *multi-tiered systems of support* (MTSS), the RTI or MTSS approach is a multitiered instructional framework that seeks to provide high-quality instruction to students with a range of needs and to monitor children's learning progress (Greenwood et al., 2012). MTSS seeks to promptly identify children who are falling behind their peers developmentally and then to provide them with instruction that is sufficient for them to catch up. Applications of tiered intervention models, particularly in the area of reading instruction, have been shown to be more effective than traditional approaches (e.g., O'Connor, Harty, & Fulmer, 2005). The MTSS model provides instruction in the students' least restrictive environment, consistent with federal special education mandates (Barnett, VanDerHeyden, & Witt, 2007). In theory, by providing high-quality instruction to all students before they fall behind, the number of students labeled with a disability will decrease (Fuchs & Fuchs, 2006).

MTSS typically is represented graphically as a triangle or a pyramid divided into three or more tiers (e.g., Fletcher & Vaughn, 2009). These tiers signify levels of increasingly intense instruction (moving up the triangle). Fewer children within a classroom are expected to need more intense instruction moving up the triangle. Thus, the lowest level of instruction (Tier 1) represents the general education curriculum that applies to all children. In contrast, the peak of the triangle (Tier 3) represents the most intense, individualized services, which is reserved for those few children for whom other services did not result in adequate progress. Between Tiers 1 and 3 is a secondary tier of instruction, intended for children who need additional support (Gersten et al., 2008). Children whose progress in Tier 1 does not meet an expected level based on screening and progress monitoring data should receive daily small group instruction (i.e., Tier 2; Fletcher & Vaughn, 2009). Thus, the *Story Friends* approach was developed primarily as a Tier 2 intervention for children demonstrating delays in oral language development.

Pedagogical Approach

Story Friends is an evidence-based early language curriculum that specifically targets vocabulary development; basic concepts; and an important component of comprehension, answering inferential questions about stories. *Story Friends* was developed as an easy-to-implement standard treatment protocol delivered to small groups, which also can be adapted for individualized intervention for preschool students. This supplemental curriculum was designed specifically for school personnel to implement in an MTSS framework.

Within the broad domain of oral language, we identified two primary areas for intervention: vocabulary and comprehension. Our first presumption was that teaching vocabulary and comprehension could be accomplished in the context of a commonly accepted preschool activity: storybook reading. This decision was based on the substantial evidence that instruction embedded in storybooks could be effective in teaching oral language skills to children (Coyne, Simmons, Kame'enui, & Stoolmiller, 2004; Ezell & Justice, 2005; Whitehurst et al., 1994; Ziolkowski & Goldstein, 2008). Although reading to students is commonplace in most preschools, there is little reason to assume that reading, even when accompanied by large or small group discussions with the children, is sufficient to greatly expand children's vocabularies and story comprehension skills. Nevertheless, the storybook context likely would be perceived positively and facilitate intervention adoption in pre-K and kindergarten settings.

A second presumption was that implementation of a Tier 2 curriculum needed to be feasible and usable in a variety of early childhood education (ECE) settings. In the context of an MTSS model, it is important to consider the demands placed on educational staff to implement multiple tiers of intervention in several domains with high treatment fidelity (Ukrainetz, 2006). Given the demands of ECE settings, the variability in the preparation of early childhood educators, and the limited time available for preparing and delivering explicit instruction, a number of design constraints need to be considered. Thus, the design of *Story Friends* was based on the premise that early childhood teachers need a curriculum that does not require extensive time for training, preparation, or implementation.

The use of recorded storybooks is a common practice, and many classrooms already have a "listening center" in place. However, exposure to books alone does not produce efficient learning of vocabulary. Therefore, it is important to provide each child who needs supplemental instruction with many opportunities to respond within an easy-to-implement enhancement on the typical preschool day. This need is met through an automated format for delivery of the curriculum. Prerecorded audio files of the story text and embedded instruction allow children wearing headphones to listen to the audio in small groups. This automated format lessens the planning burden for teachers because it reduces the variation in teachers' ability to select words, generate child-friendly definitions, and develop story contexts for teaching vocabulary. Plus, aides or volunteers can implement the curriculum with high fidelity in ECE settings. The prerecorded books with embedded lessons help ensure consistent delivery and dosage of instruction. That is, each child, equipped with a book and headphones, receives specific lessons and multiple opportunities to respond. However, adults do more than simply push *play*. We have found that an adult facilitator needs to keep children on the right page and to encourage responding. However, an adult with minimal training, rather than a highly skilled teacher, could facilitate this type of small group instruction because carefully designed instruction is provided in the prerecorded audio.

Thus, we developed, tested, and refined a supplemental language curriculum in which instruction teaches relevant skills, produces learning efficiently, and can be implemented easily by adults with varying levels of teaching skills. Storybooks were created to meet these design characteristics:

- Books are appealing to young children and their teachers.
- Each book series has a recurring cast of characters, thus reducing demands on learning background information in single books.
- A few appealing characters per book series are depicted in colorful illustrations.
- Each page includes rhyming text to facilitate learning of an aspect of phonological awareness.
- Stories provide a rich context for embedded intervention on vocabulary and comprehension.
- Vocabulary and linguistic complexity, as well as the number of pages, is controlled and consistent.
- Child-friendly themes and morals provide a basis for each story.

The *Story Friends* curriculum was developed by the Center for Response to Intervention in Early Childhood (CRTIEC), a multisite collaborative project funded by the Institute of Educational Sciences. This intervention has been used successfully in multiple research studies with pre-K students who are at risk for reading disabilities due to delays in vocabulary development. Previous research has found that students vary in their daily language exposure and that many children benefit from explicit instruction on vocabulary words and comprehension strategies. As discussed below, using Individual Growth and Development Indicators (IGDIs, McConnell, Bradfield, Wackerle-Hollman, & Rodriguez, 2015) and teacher questionnaires, children who require extra support can be identified as potential candidates for intervention.

Students who benefit most from *Story Friends* instruction are those who are not sustaining typical growth in the areas of language and literacy. Students selected for participation in previous studies are children demonstrating language delays on both IGDIs. The IGDI 2.0 Picture Naming and Which One Doesn't Belong subtests, along with a teacher questionnaire, have been shown to be effective in identifying preschoolers who demonstrate delays in vocabulary and comprehension skills but have sufficient core vocabulary to understand the definitions and the stories (Bradfield et al., 2013). At 3-week intervals and after a review book, unit tests provide performance data for informing the MTSS framework and determining whether adjustments to the tiers of instruction are warranted. For example, a child who is able to define all or most of the challenging words and answer inferential questions would not be considered a high priority for continuing to receive *Story Friends.* Alternatively, a child who is unable to define any or few of the challenging words or answer inferential questions might benefit from an individualized adaptation of *Story Friends* or from instruction on a less advanced set of language goals.

The *Story Friends* curriculum consists of a total of 26 storybooks (two sets of 13). Each child has a book because the books have interactive activities, such as flaps that children lift to reveal answers to questions. Typically, groups of three children listen simultaneously to each automated storybook three times per week, with each lesson lasting approximately 10–15 minutes. Each set (*Jungle Friends* and *Forest Friends*) has one introductory book, nine books with new vocabulary and comprehension content, and three review books. Children are led through the stories by "Wanda the Word Wolf," who narrates the book, defines the vocabulary and basic concept words, provides opportunities for practice, and asks comprehension questions that allow children to apply concepts from the stories to their own lives. Children learn two new challenging academic words and one or more basic concept words per story and have opportunities to practice these newly learned words at the end of each book. The books are organized into units of three stories. Thus, children listen to three books and then listen to a fourth book that reviews the words that were taught previously.

Research

Although many curricula claim to be evidence-based, few have conducted multiple studies to inform the curriculum development process and systematically scaled up the research to ensure that intervention effects are replicated in authentic classroom contexts. This research overview summarizes much of the research conducted thus far that has built a strong evidence base for the *Story Friends* curriculum. In addition to initial pilot work, five experimental studies using the *Story Friends* curriculum were conducted between 2010 and 2014.

1. Spencer et al. (2012) reported the results of an early efficacy study of this embedded vocabulary intervention. A repeated acquisition single-case experimental design across instructional targets was used. Robust experimental effects were replicated across nine children in public pre-K classrooms serving low-income families.

2. A subsequent study (Kelley, Goldstein, Spencer, & Sherman, 2015) used a small n group design and an embedded single-case experimental design. Eighteen participants were randomly assigned to treatment (nine books in the fall) or delayed treatment (nine books in the spring) within classrooms. Even stronger evidence of efficacy was demonstrated in this study. Large effect sizes were evident across the three units (range, $d = 1.37–2.62$). Improvements in vocabulary knowledge were demonstrated in 58 of 81 possible demonstrations of treatment effects. On average, children in the treatment group learned approximately 52% of the words compared to 5% for the comparison group. The results on Assessment of Story Comprehension were not as impressive, overall; however, a large effect size was seen at posttest for the inferential questions ($d = 1.10$).

3. These results were replicated in a study that was conducted in Kansas City at the same time (Greenwood et al., in press). This study focused on children's responses to the narrator's prompts. They found that children improved in their proficiency in responding to the prerecorded narrator. These improvements in correct responding to teaching prompts were associated with increases in word learning.

4. Goldstein et al. (in press) reported on a large-scale study with teaching staff implementing the *Story Friends* curriculum. This multisite study included 195 students in 32 classrooms across two states. Classroom–student clusters were randomly assigned to one of the two conditions. In the experimental condition, the storybooks and audio included embedded lessons on challenging vocabulary words and comprehension questions. In the comparison condition, participants were exposed to the same stories with the targeted vocabulary words included but with no embedded lessons. To identify participants, we considered information from the Picture Naming and Which One Doesn't Belong IGDIs and teacher nomination on Teacher Questionnaires. Children with low scores on one or both IGDIs also were given the PPVT-4.

Learning of instructional targets was assessed using two curriculum-based measures referenced to the new content taught: Unit Vocabulary Tests and the Assessment of Story Comprehension (ASC, T. D. Spencer, Goldstein, Kelley, Sherman, & McCune, 2015). Children in both conditions showed little knowledge of the novel words at pretest. This did not change at posttest for the comparison group after being exposed to the words in story contexts. However, word learning was quite evident at posttest for the experimental group. After controlling for pretest vocabulary scores and Clinical Evaluation of Language Fundamentals (CELF-P2, Wiig, Secord, & Semel, 2004) scores, a large effect for group was evident (Cohen's $f^2 = .70$). Overall effects for the ASC were not significant in this study. This study contributes greatly to the internal validity of findings because the basis of comparison was listening to books with the targeted vocabulary included. Vocabulary learning associated with embedded learning was shown along with a large effect size. It also contributes to the external validity of our findings, because teachers were responsible for implementing the curriculum. They did so with excellent treatment fidelity and with high consumer satisfaction.

A second cluster-randomized design, using ECE teachers as implementers, was conducted recently with 39 child care centers in three states. In this study, students were randomized to an embedded vocabulary condition (*Story Friends*) or a phonological awareness condition. Children in both groups were provided instruction for approximately 15 minutes per day for approximately 12 weeks. Teachers in ECE centers were trained by research staff to implement the interventions, and coaching support was provided on a weekly basis. Fidelity observations indicated a high degree of fidelity to each program with little researcher support. Despite minimal training and classroom support by research staff, previous results were replicated. Children learned an average of 46% of 18 challenging target words over the course of the 12-week intervention versus 7% for the comparison group.

In summary, the five studies conducted between 2010 and 2014 allowed us to evaluate and refine the *Story Friends* curriculum. Kelley and Goldstein (2014) provide a more complete overview of curricular development process. Refinements in the curriculum were based on careful analyses of students' learning across sites. These changes have produced more robust learning by preschoolers, especially for the learning of academic vocabulary. Moreover, we have consistently found that the *Story Friends* curriculum was easy to implement, worked well with current class curricula, and resulted in substantial word-learning gains even when children are exposed to the words in story contexts but without the embedded lessons. The long-term effects of this curriculum have yet to be investigated experimentally (although preliminary results from kindergarten readiness tests look promising). Because vocabulary development is clearly implicated in later reading fluency and comprehension, longitudinal studies are needed to determine long-term effects on later reading development.

REFERENCES

Barnett, D.W., VanDerHeyden, A.M., & Witt, J.C. (2007). Achieving science-based practice through response to intervention: What it might look like in preschools. *Journal of Educational and Psychological Consultation, 17*, 31–54.

Bradfield, T. A., Besner, A. C., Wackerle-Hollman, A. K., Albano, A. D., Rodriguez, M. C., & McConnell, S. R. (2014). Redefining individual growth and development indicators: Oral language. *Assessment for Effective Intervention, 39*(4), 233–244. doi:10.1177/1534508413496837

Coyne, M.D., Simmons, D.C., Kame'enui, E.J., & Stoolmiller, M. (2004). Teaching vocabulary during shared storybook readings: An examination of differential effects. *Exceptionality, 12*(3), 145–162.

Dunn, L.M., & Dunn, L.M. (1997). *Peabody Picture Vocabulary Test–Third Edition (PPVT-III).* Circle Pines, MN: American Guidance Service.

Ezell, H.K., & Justice, L.M. (2005). *Shared storybook reading: Building young children's language & emergent literacy skills.* Baltimore, MD: Paul H. Brookes Publishing Co.

Fletcher, J., & Vaughn, S. (2009). Response to Intervention: Preventing and remediating academic difficulties. *Child Development Perspectives, 3*(1), 30–37.

Foster, W.A., & Miller, M. (2007). Development of the literacy achievement gap: A longitudinal study of kindergarten through third grade. *Language, Speech, and Hearing Services in Schools, 38*(3), 173–181.

Fuchs, D., & Fuchs, L.S. (2006). Introduction to response to intervention: What, why, and how valid is it? *Reading Research Quarterly, 41,* 93–99.

Gersten, R., Compton, D., Connor, C.M., Dimino, J., Santoro, L., Linan-Thompson, S., & Tilly, W.D. (2008). *Assisting students struggling with reading: Response to Intervention and multi-tier intervention for reading in the primary grades. A practice guide.* (NCEE 2009-4045). Washington, DC: National Center for Education Evaluation and Regional Assistance, Institute of Education Sciences, U.S. Department of Education.

Goldstein, H., Kelley, E.S., Greenwood, C.R., McCune, L., Carta, J., Atwater, J., . . . Spencer, T. (in press). Embedded instruction improves vocabulary learning during automated storybook reading among high-risk preschoolers. *Journal of Speech, Language, and Hearing Research.*

Greenwood, C.R., Carta, J.J., Atwater, J., Goldstein, H., Kaminski, R., & McConnell, S.R. (2012). Is a response to intervention (RTI) approach to preschool language and early literacy instruction needed? *Topics in Early Childhood Special Education, 33*(8), 48–64.

Greenwood, C.R., Carta, J.J., Kelley, E.S., Guerrero, G., Kong, N.Y., Atwater, J., & Goldstein, H. (in press). Systematic replication of the effects of a supplementary, technology-assisted, storybook intervention for preschool children with weak vocabulary and comprehension skills. *The Elementary School Journal.*

Kelley, E.S., & Goldstein, H. (2014). Building a Tier 2 intervention: A glimpse behind the data. *Journal of Early Intervention, 36*(4), 292–312. doi:10.1177/1053815115581657

Kelley, E.S., Goldstein, H., Spencer, T., & Sherman, A. (2015). Effects of automated Tier 2 storybook intervention on vocabulary and comprehension learning in preschool children with limited oral language skills. *Early Childhood Research Quarterly, 31,* 47–61. doi:10.1016/j.ecresq.2014.12.004

McConnell, S., Bradfield, T., Wackerle-Hollman, A., & Rodriguez, M. (2015). *Individual Growth and Development Indicators of Early Literacy* (2nd ed.-Universal Screening ed.). Saint Paul, MN: Early Learning Labs.

National Center for Education Statistics. (2014). *The nation's report card: Are the nation's 12th-graders making progress in mathematics and reading?* (NCES 2014-087). Washington, DC: Institute of Education Sciences, U.S. Department of Education.

National Early Literacy Panel. (2008). *Developing Early Literacy: Report of the National Early Literacy Panel.* Washington, DC: National Institute for Literacy.

O'Connor, R.E., Harty, K.R., & Fulmer, D. (2005). Tiers of intervention in kindergarten through third grade. *Journal of Learning Disabilities, 38,* 532–538.

Qi, C. H., Kaiser, A. P., Milan, S., & Hancock, T. (2006). Language performance of low-income African American and European American preschool children on the PPVT-III. *Language, Speech, and Hearing Services in Schools, 37,* 5-16. doi: 0161-1461/06/3701-0005

Spencer, E.J., Goldstein, H., Sherman, A., Noe, S., Tabbah, R., Ziolkowski, R., & Schneider, N. (2012). Effects of an automated vocabulary and comprehension intervention: An early efficacy study. *Journal of Early Intervention, 34,* 195–221.

Spencer, T. D., Goldstein, H., Kelley, E. S., Sherman, A., & McCune, L. (2015). A curriculum-based measure of language comprehension for preschoolers: Reliability and validity of the Assessment of Story Comprehension (ASC). *Manuscript submitted for publication.*

Ukrainetz, T.A. (2006). The implications of RTI and EBP for SLPs: Commentary on L.M. Justice. *Language Speech and Hearing Services in Schools, 37,* 298–303.

Whitehurst, G., Arnold, D., Epstein, J., Angell, A., Smith, M., & Fischell, J. (1994). A picture book reading intervention in day care and home for children from low-income families. *Developmental Psychology, 30,* 679–689.

Wiig, E. H., Secord, W. A., & Semel, E. (2004). *Clinical Evaluation of Language Fundamentals Preschool-Second Edition.* San Antonio, TX: Pearson Assessments.

Ziolkowski, R.A., & Goldstein, H. (2008). Effects of an embedded phonological awareness intervention during repeated book reading on preschool children with language delays. *Journal of Early Intervention, 31*(1), 67–90.